hew Robertson is a London-based bartender with over 17 years'
rience. He now works for events and creative consultancy Heads, Hearts
Tails, delivering drinks development and education to the hospitality
stry, global spirit brands and most importantly, people. He is very good
opping things, and finds almost all machinery problematic.

buted in the US by
ette Book Group
Avenue of the Americas
nd 5th Floors
York, NY 10104

buted in Canada by
dian Manda Group
nnette St.
to, Ontario, Canada M6S 2C8

achette UK Company
hachette.co.uk

ublished in Great Britain in 2018 by Hamlyn,
sion of Octopus Publishing Group Ltd
elite House, 50 Victoria Embankment, London EC4Y 0DZ
octopusbooks.co.uk

978-0-7537-3306-6

catalogue record for this book is available from the British Library

d and bound in China

er: Lucy Pessell
: Lucy Pessell
Sarah Vaughan
buting Editor: Matthew Robertson
acknowledgments: © Alexander Suricoma Babich; 123RF/suricoma; Dreamstime.com/suricoma_info

sure that has been used in the recipes is based on a bar jigger, which is 25 ml (1 fl oz).
red, a different volume can be used, providing the proportions are kept constant within
nd suitable adjustments are made to spoon measurements, where they occur.

d level spoon measurements are used in all recipes.
oon = one 15 ml spoon
on = one 5 ml spoon

k contains cocktails made with raw or lightly cooked eggs. It is prudent for more
le people to avoid uncooked or lightly cooked cocktails made with eggs.

k includes cocktails made with nuts and nut derivatives. It is advisable for customers
wn allergic reactions to nuts and nut derivatives and those who may be potentially
le to these allergies, to avoid these recipes. It is also prudent to check the labels of
ared ingredients for the possible inclusion of nut derivatives.

this material previously appeared in *501 Must-Drink Cocktails* and *Hamlyn All Colour
200 Classic Cocktails*.

THE
COCKTAIL
BIBLE

AN A–Z OF **TWO HUNDRED CLA**
AND **CONTEMPORARY COCKT**

WITH **ANECDOTES** FOR THE **CURIOUS**
TECHNIQUES FOR THE **ADVENTU**

Ma
exp
and
indi
at a

Dist
Hac
129
4th
New

Dist
Can
664
Toro

An I
www

First
a div
Carr
www

Cop

All r
elect
syste

ISBN

A CI

Prin

10 9

Publ
Desig
Edito
Cont
Pictu

The n
If pref
a drin

Standa
1 table
1 teasp

This b
vulner

This b
with kr
vulnera
pre-pre

Some c
Cooker

THE
COCKTAIL
BIBLE

**MATTHEW
ROBERTSON**

hamlyn

CONTENTS

INTRODUCTION

As with any cultural curiosity that drifts in and out of fashion, it feels right now that we have discovered something completely new. But cocktails and mixed drinks have always been here. From punches to Sours, Martinis to Spritzes, their origins date back centuries. They were derived from simple shared concepts, and then built upon by proceeding generations as time passed, demand evolved and tastes shifted. Aside from being adventurous, delicious, evocative, fun and sociable, they are fascinating. The things that go into them and the reasons they came to be are of genuine interest to anybody. Each individual drink, each spirit or liqueur, each piece of glassware, contains a history lesson in itself.

Drinks are symbols. Though they are made of liquid, and drunk from a vessel of one form or another, they are not just a collection of materials. They have meaning, they carry stories and they mark time. That time might have been a solely specific moment, or a particular drink might be more loosely reflective of the point in history that it was created. Or they can be present-day celebrations, occasions. A wedding, an anniversary, a promotion, a beginning or an ending. Maybe it's just the end of the day in a bar with somebody you love.

But they are not only markers of time. They are expressions of hard work, clarity of vision and refinement of process. They contain ideas, they were created by people, are made by people and (unless like me you're from the south west of England where even the ducks drink cider) they are consumed by people.

The making of things – in this case a simple mixed drink – can actually have broader personal applications. By assembling a cocktail at home with care, attention and no little affection, we can connect simply and directly with that most magical and elusive of human endeavours – personal process. That engagement with process, like any craft-based activity, can provide us with a satisfaction that will only permeate positively into other areas of our lives.

But what are cocktails? "A stimulating liquor, composed of spirits of any kind, sugar, water and bitters" said the American writer Harry Croswell in 1806. Wholly true, and taken loosely, that description is the basis of all mixed drinks. But the idea of the cocktail is a wildly appropriated notion to start with. Bartenders or (yawn) mixologists were the original fusion chefs. It is rare in cookery that you would put barley from Scotland, grapes from Italy and cloves from Trinidad and Tobago on the same plate – in fact you'd most likely be moved to the silly section of the kitchen if you did. But barley makes whisky, grapes make sweet vermouth, Angostura bitters are made from cloves, and their sum parts were judiciously combined at the Waldorf Astoria in New York City in 1894 to create the Rob Roy cocktail, a drink exemplifying the very virtues of balance and nuanced harmony. With cocktails, the rules are a bit different. That being said, locality will always factor, as historically what was grown, produced or imported nearest-by would most probably have ended up in the drink.

When it comes to how we do it, whether we are creating something completely new or re-interpreting an age-old standard, we always strive for balance. Complementary combinations, layered with complexity and balanced with simplicity. The basis of classical cocktail-making lies in the balance between sweet and sour. That balance is expressed most commonly through citrus juice and sugar, the building blocks of a drink upon which nearly all the classics sit. So, after a while you will notice recurring themes. A spirit, a citrus element and a sweet element. After that, those base components could be augmented with a modifier; the sweet element might become a liqueur, or the citrus might become a softer fruit juice used to lengthen a drink while retaining sharpness. Teas or wines could be added to give background complexity. On and on it goes. May it never end.

The thing to remember is this. The development and delivery of food and drink reside in an endlessly contradictory halfway house of strictly measured and repeated precision, and the unmeasurable sense of the "felt". The recipe may be the recipe, and it may be a hundred years old, but if you feel on a wet Wednesday that you need a dash more lime juice in your Daiquiri, then that really is your decision, and that feeling should be responded to, and that is how it should always be.

"If you don't state a clear preference, then your drink is like a bad game of poker or a hasty drug transaction: It is whatever the dealer says it is. Please do try to bear this in mind."

Christopher Hitchens, *Everyday Drinking*

TECHNIQUE
AND METHOD

A guide to the equipment and techniques that are used, not only in this book, but in bars of note all over the world. Even the simplest drinks require a preparation of sorts, but cocktails can present some potentially intimidating challenges. There are pieces of kit, there are tools, there are measurements, there are dry ingredients and liquid ingredients; there is the weight of hundreds of years of history and, to cap it all off, there is Tom Cruise throwing bottles around behind bars in films to contend with too. But in truth it's really quite simple. Making a cocktail is just like anything else where a process needs to be engaged with or instructions need to be followed; it is as difficult as you make it.

Do remember to have fun.

SHAKING

Shaking is the most universally recognizable way of preparing a drink. We shake a cocktail for four reasons: to mix it, to chill it, to dilute it and to create texture through aeration. Generally speaking there are two types of cocktail shaker commonly used: the three-part shaker (or **COBBLER SHAKER***) and the two-part shaker (or* **BOSTON SHAKER***).*

For our purposes, the method will always be the same. Always use good-quality, completely frozen cubes of ice, never cracked or crushed.

IF USING A **THREE-PART SHAKER***:* Add your ingredients to the bottom piece and two-thirds fill with ice, affix the other two pieces and shake vigorously for 5–10 seconds.

IF USING A **TWO-PART SHAKER***:* Add the ingredients to the glass or smaller part of your shaker, and then two-thirds fill the larger part with ice. Bring the two parts together, clasp firmly with both hands and shake vigorously for 5–10 seconds.

DRY SHAKING

We whip or "dry shake" a cocktail without ice to incorporate egg whites into the drink, and to create a luxuriously fluffy texture and mouth feel, usually in a Sour or a Fizz. This binds the mixture together, so once we have "dry shaken", we then need to shake again but this time with ice, as you would with any other shaken drink.

STIRRING

Stirring is a gentler way of mixing and chilling a cocktail while at the same time creating a smooth liquid texture, almost oil-like in its viscosity. The aim is to avoid chipping or cracking the ice as you stir, as the tiny flecks you chip off will add unwanted dilution to your drink.

To best control temperature and dilution with stirred drinks, unless suggested otherwise, always add the ingredients first, then fill a cocktail shaker or mixing glass (if you have one) with cubed ice, and stir gently but purposefully with a bar spoon for 30 seconds.

STRAINING

After shaking or stirring, we need to strain the drink so that the chipped ice and anything else left in the shaker, like herbs or fruit, do not end up in the final drink.

If you are using a three-part shaker, you will have a strainer built-in, but with a two-part shaker you will need a cocktail strainer, which is clasped over the top before pouring the drink into the glass.

DOUBLE STRAINING

For any drink served "up" or without ice, like a Daiquiri, strain additionally through a small sieve or tea strainer to ensure that absolutely nothing that was in the shaker or mixing glass ends up in the drink. We always want to taste the ingredients, but sometimes we don't want to see them.

MUDDLING

To best the extract juices and skin oils from herbs and fruit, we muddle them, by crushing them in the base of the glass or cocktail shaker. Muddlers can be found in shops quite easily, but a standard rolling pin does the job just as well.

CHURNING

Churning is the technique of combining dry and liquid ingredients with crushed ice within the glass, as with drinks such as the Mojito, and is often a process that follows muddling.

It is best achieved by vigorously mixing the ingredients and crushed ice with a long-handled bar spoon for 5–10 seconds.

MEASURING

Always measure your ingredients. Always. For this you will need a cocktail measure, or what might be otherwise known as a jigger (shortened from the silly but wholly logical original term for a measure, a "thing-a-ma-jigger"), which are readily available to buy. Measuring accurately is so important in creating consistent drinks time and time again and as the original recipe intended. To put it in a culinary context: you would never ignore the specifically stated measurements when baking a cake as something would most likely go awry along the way if you did; so neither should you when making a cocktail, however

tempting it might be to sling in that extra measure of gin...! It's a question of flavour balance – the recipes state measurements for a reason, and getting that balance right will make your drink all the better.

BLENDING

Blending allows us to incorporate ice completely into a drink, creating a smooth Frappé-like texture.

You can do this in a domestic blender or food processor.

ICE

Strange as it may seem, ice is the most important component of any mixed drink. Ice is your best friend, so please make sure you have plenty of it. It chills liquid to the desired temperature, it dilutes, and it softens the rougher edges of strong spirits. Ice is just as important in the making and serving of a cocktail as any other ingredient listed in the recipe, so good-quality ice must be a mainstay of any home bar. Shop-bought ice cubes are great, though as a last resort homemade ice made in freezer trays will of course do.

On the occasions where a recipe calls for crushed ice, if

you have a fancy ice-crushing contraption, lovely, but wrapping cubed ice in a tea towel and bashing the daylights out of it with a rolling pin or unwanted ornament will give you exactly the same result.

INGREDIENTS

To start, a basic larder of reasonable quality vodka, gin, light and dark rum, tequila, bourbon, rye whiskey and Scottish whisky will give you a solid platform from which to build. Add to this the most commonly used liqueurs or modifiers, which would be an orange liqueur or triple sec (Cointreau being the most readily available), sweet and dry Italian vermouths, and maraschino, and you will find yourself in a place of surprising readiness to create dozens of classic and contemporary cocktails. After this, any studied addition to your collection will be a worthwhile one.

It is worth noting that in these times of great spirit innovation and collective enthusiasm, particularly within the world of gin, there are now countless creative and experimental expressions of the classic spirit categories available to us, and the recipes that follow are rooted in somewhat simpler times. So, while every new product out there should be cherished and enjoyed, try and keep it simple and classic in your base spirit selection when it comes to cocktail creation.

JUICE

All citrus juice must, without exception, be freshly squeezed. If you use shop-bought, pasteurized products, your drinks will quite simply taste revolting. Time consuming though it may be, it really is the only way to do it. When it comes to other fruit juices, whether you do it yourself or buy them, freshly pressed juice will always taste better.

SYRUPS

All the syrups we use in this book can be easily sourced in shops and supermarkets, even sugar syrup. However, you may wish to make your own. The recipes that contain sugar syrup, and there are many, are based on an equal parts (1:1) sugar to water ratio.

To make 500ml of sugar syrup, combine 300ml warm water and 300g caster sugar, and stir until the sugar has completely dissolved.

Something to consider is that shop-bought syrups tend to be much sweeter, often nearing a 2:1 sugar to water ratio – so if you are using a pre-made product, in which there is no shame whatsoever, you may wish to reduce the amount of sugar syrup you add to your cocktails. Flavour is subjective – the best judge of what tastes right will always be you.

GARNISHING

Eating and drinking are experiences that engage all the senses, and the first sense we usually engage is sight. We literally drink with our eyes. Decorating or garnishing a drink attractively instantly makes it more appealing. Garnishes will also add to the drink's aroma, often creating a contrasting flavour profile. And if something looks great and smells great, it probably tastes great.

The most common garnish we will use is citrus fruit. Lemons, limes, oranges and grapefruit can be cut into wedges or half-moon slices, or their peel can be cut off and used as "twists".

To prepare a twist, we slice the peel off the fruit with a paring knife or vegetable peeler. Don't worry if you take the pith along with the peel, you can carefully slice that off afterwards. If you wish, you can cut it into a fancy or decorative shape, but leaving it rugged and natural looking is just as appealing in its own way. Once ready to use, gently squeeze the twist over the top of the liquid to express the oils in the skin, and unless instructed to discard it, drop it into the drink.

It goes without saying that using the freshest and best-quality fruit you possibly can will give you the best results.

GLASSWARE

Though ultimately functional, glasses are also beautiful things. Be they antique or contemporary, they are iconic and unique. They are often also deeply personal objects, as most of us have in our possession a single vessel or a set of something or other that was passed down or given to us, and in them lie stories. In this book we suggest the appropriate glassware for each cocktail – but with a little imagination tempered with a modicum of common sense, the selections herein can to an extent easily be interchanged. Common sense though is the key; if your antique set of hurricane glasses was destroyed in some sort of freak weather incident, a highball glass will happily do the job, but a line might be drawn at swapping a Champagne flute for a pint glass for reasons far too obvious to list here.

CHAMPAGNE FLUTE

Long and elegant, and developed in the 1700s. The extended height and surface area help to stop air escaping, and so retain a sparking wine's carbonation for longer.

COUPETTE

Predating the Martini glass by roughly several hundred years, a popular misconception is that the coupette was modelled on the shape of one of the French Queen Marie-Antoinette's breasts. However, the Champagne coupette was in fact developed in England over a hundred years prior to this, and so debunks such saucy nonsense. Identical to the Martini glass in form, its greatest and everlasting benefit is its narrower aperture, which saves many a

spill caused by a waywardly
gesticulating arm.

HIGHBALL

Another name for a tall tumbler
glass. The ideal vessel for long
drinks, allowing plenty of room for
liquid and ice.

HURRICANE

A large highball glass, with a
curved shape not unlike a lamp.
Used for drinks such as the Piña
Colada and, unsurprisingly, the
Hurricane.

MARGARITA GLASS

A fun extension of the Champagne
coupette, wide brimmed to best
hold salt and a lime wedge. When
viewed from a particular angle,
and after a few Margaritas, one
might argue that it looks a bit like
an upside-down sombrero. Might
being the operative word…

MARTINI

The iconic cocktail glass. Long-
stemmed so that the temperature of

*the short drink contained within it
would not be spoiled by hot hands,
and aromatics from the spirit and
garnish could be best enjoyed from
its outwardly tapering edge. First
presented at the Paris Exhibition
of 1925, it is the epitome of Art
Deco elegance.*

OLD-FASHIONED
*Identical to the rocks glass, but
usually more decorative in design
or shape. Pleasant to look at and
satisfying to hold.*

ROCKS
*A short lowball glass, for drinks
with less liquid volume or drinks
that are served without ice, or neat.*

SHOT GLASS
*For chinning shots out of well
quickly.*

A

ABC Cocktail

A classic combination of Cognac and port; the mint brings a welcome freshness to this rich aperitif.

1 MEASURE COGNAC

1 MEASURE TAWNY PORT

3 TSP MARASCHINO

1 TSP SUGAR SYRUP

6 MINT LEAVES, PLUS AN EXTRA

LEAF TO GARNISH

Add all the ingredients to your cocktail shaker. Shake vigorously and double strain into a Martini glass. Garnish with a mint leaf.

ABSINTHE
Originating in Switzerland in the late 1800s, absinthe is a distilled and highly alcoholic anise-flavoured spirit, including botanicals of flowers and Artemisia absinthium (wormwood). It rose to great popularity in

late 19th-century France, being a particular favourite of the Parisian bohemian set – with James Joyce, Henri de Toulouse-Lautrec and Ernest Hemingway as noted absinthe drinkers.

ADA COLEMAN

Ada "Coley" Coleman (1875–1966), was head bartender (and the first woman to fill the role) at the American Bar of London's Savoy Hotel, where she worked for 23 years. Such was her popularity with customers, her retirement was announced in national newspapers. Her most enduring recipe is that of the Hanky Panky, reportedly created for the actor Charles Hawtrey.

AGAVE JULEP

Giving the Kentucky Derby classic a Mexican twist. Grassy, herbaceous tequila and sweet agave combine beautifully to create a bracing mid-afternoon tipple.

2 MEASURES BLANCO TEQUILA

¾ MEASURE LIME JUICE

2 TSP AGAVE SYRUP

8 MINT LEAVES

MINT SPRIG, TO GARNISH

Add all the ingredients to a highball glass.
Fill the glass with crushed ice, and churn.
Top up with more crushed ice.
Garnish with a mint sprig.

AIRMAIL

Said to have been created in Cuba to celebrate the arrival of air-delivered mail to the island, this is a superb Daiquiri variation crisply enlivened by Champagne.

1 MEASURE RUM
½ MEASURE LIME JUICE
½ MEASURE HONEY
CHILLED CHAMPAGNE, TO TOP

Add the rum, lime and honey
to your cocktail shaker.
Shake with cubed ice,
double strain into a
Champagne flute, and
top with Champagne.
No garnish.

ALGONQUIN

*A fantastic whiskey snifter with
a tropical twist. Named after the
notorious hotel in mid-town
Manhattan, where it was first
served in the 1930s.*

1¼ MEASURES RYE WHISKEY
½ MEASURE DRY VERMOUTH
1 MEASURE PINEAPPLE JUICE
COCKTAIL CHERRY, TO
GARNISH

Add all the ingredients to
your cocktail shaker.
Shake vigorously and double

strain into a chilled coupette
glass.
Garnish with a cocktail
cherry.

AMARETTO SOUR

*A more complex version of the
contemporary favourite, with
Scotch whisky added to balance
the extreme sweetness of
Amaretto.*

1½ MEASURES AMARETTO
½ MEASURE BLENDED SCOTCH
WHISKY
1 MEASURE LEMON JUICE
½ MEASURE SUGAR SYRUP
½ MEASURE EGG WHITE
TO GARNISH
LEMON WEDGE
COCKTAIL CHERRY

Add all the ingredients to
your cocktail shaker and
vigorously "dry shake"
without ice for 10 seconds.
Take the shaker apart,
add cubed ice and shake
vigorously.

Strain into an old-fashioned glass filled with cubed ice. Garnish with a lemon wedge and a cocktail cherry.

AMERICANO

Predating the Negroni, the Americano is the most classic of Italian aperitivos. Halfway between a Spritz and a Collins, its relatively low potency means that three or four can be enjoyed in one sitting. Simple, timeless and unmatchable.

1 MEASURE CAMPARI

1 MEASURE SWEET VERMOUTH

SODA WATER, TO TOP

ORANGE SLICE, TO GARNISH

Fill a highball glass with cubed ice, add the Campari and sweet vermouth, stir and top with soda water. Garnish with an orange slice.

APEROL SPRITZ

Summer has not begun until the first Aperol Spritz has been sipped. Soft and delicate, crisp Prosecco offsets Aperol's gentle rhubarb-laced sweetness.

3 MEASURES CHILLED PROSECCO

2 MEASURES APEROL

1 MEASURE SODA WATER

ORANGE SLICE, TO GARNISH

Fill a wine glass with cubed ice and add the Prosecco and Aperol. Stir briefly and add the soda water. Garnish with an orange slice.

APPLEJACK SOUR

Crisp and tart. A complex Sour for those with a drier palate.

2 MEASURES APPLE BRANDY

1 MEASURE LEMON JUICE

¾ MEASURE SUGAR SYRUP

TO GARNISH

APPLE SLICES

LEMON WEDGE

Add all the ingredients to your cocktail shaker.
Shake and double strain into a rocks glass.
Garnish with slices of apple and a lemon wedge.

APPLE MARTINI

Maligned and loved, the Apple Martini rightly deserves its place as a modern classic. Sharp, sour and ice cold.

1¾ MEASURES VODKA

¾ MEASURE APPLE SCHNAPPS

1 MEASURE APPLE JUICE

½ MEASURE LIME JUICE

½ MEASURE LEMON JUICE

½ MEASURE SUGAR SYRUP

PINCH OF CINNAMON

APPLE SLICES, TO GARNISH

Add all the ingredients to your cocktail shaker.
Shake vigorously and double strain into a chilled Martini glass.
Garnish with slices of apple.

ARMY AND NAVY

A Gin Sour, flavoured with almond. This can be fiendishly difficult to balance, so ensure you measure your ingredients accurately and shake well.

2 MEASURES GIN

1 MEASURE LEMON JUICE

½ MEASURE ORGEAT SYRUP

LEMON TWIST, TO GARNISH

Add all the ingredients to your cocktail shaker.
Shake vigorously and double strain into a chilled coupette glass.
Garnish with a lemon twist.

AVIATION

Created at the Savoy Hotel and first appearing in print in 1930, Aviation is another of its creator, Harry Craddock's, endless and innovative variations on the Gin Sour – elegantly balancing gin and lemon with bitter cherry and perfumed violet. Easy when you know how.

1¾ MEASURES GIN

½ MEASURE LEMON JUICE

¼ MEASURE MARASCHINO

¼ MEASURE CRÈME DE VIOLETTE

COCKTAIL CHERRY, TO GARNISH

Add all the ingredients to your cocktail shaker.
Shake vigorously and double strain into a chilled coupette glass.
Garnish with a cocktail cherry.

AVONDALE HABIT

These seemingly mismatched flavours combine to complement each other wonderfully. Best served as a winter aperitif.

1½ MEASURES BRANDY

¼ MEASURE CRÈME DE MENTHE

6 MINT LEAVES

3 HULLED STRAWBERRIES, PLUS 1 EXTRA TO GARNISH

2 TSP SUGAR SYRUP

PINCH OF CRACKED BLACK PEPPER

MINT SPRIG, TO GARNISH

Muddle the strawberries in an old-fashioned glass, then add all the remaining ingredients, fill the glass with crushed ice and churn.
Top with more crushed ice and garnish with a mint sprig and a strawberry.

B

BEES KNEES

BELLINI

BENEDICT

BÉNÉDICTINE

BETWEEN THE SHEETS

BITTERS

BLINKER

BLOODY MARY

BLUE CURAÇAO

BLUE HAWAIIAN

BOBBY BURNS

BOMBAY PUNCH

BOULEVARDIER

BOURBON

BRAMBLE

BRANDY ALEXANDER

BRANDY CRUSTA

BREAKFAST MARTINI

BRITISH MOJITO

BRONX

BUCKS FIZZ

B

BEES KNEES

With its name meaning "the best", the addition of honey to this Prohibition-era favourite was a creative method of masking the dubious taste of poor quality "bathtub" gin. Floral, zingy and (if made correctly) extremely well balanced.

2 MEASURES GIN
1 MEASURE LEMON JUICE
½ MEASURE HONEY
LEMON TWIST, TO GARNISH

Add all the ingredients to your cocktail shaker.
Shake vigorously and double strain into a chilled coupette glass.
Garnish with a lemon twist.

BELLINI

Created in 1948 by Giuseppe Cipriani, owner of Harry's Bar in Venice, inspired by the 15th-century Venetian artist

Giovanni Bellini. A perfect pairing of peaches and sparkling wine, this timeless classic is enjoyed the world over.

½ RIPE WHITE PEACH

1 DASH SUGAR SYRUP

CHILLED PROSECCO, TO TOP

Add the peach and sugar syrup to a blender or food processor and blend until smooth.
Pour into a Champagne flute and top with Prosecco, ensure both ingredients are mixed together completely. No garnish.

BENEDICT

The musky and heady herbal notes of Bénédictine are a fantastic addition to a simple Scotch Highball.

1 MEASURE BÉNÉDICTINE

1 MEASURE BLENDED SCOTCH

GINGER ALE, TO TOP

LEMON WEDGE, TO GARNISH

Add the Bénédictine and the Scotch to a rocks glass filled with cubed ice.
Top up with ginger ale and garnish with a lemon wedge.

BÉNÉDICTINE
Bénédictine was created in 1863 by wine merchant Alexandre Le Grand in Fécamp, Normandy, France. He derived the recipe from early 16th-century scripture that he found, detailing a mysterious elixir produced by monks at the abbey at Fécamp. It is produced by distilling and then blending 27 herbs, spices and botanicals, giving a sweet and spiced herbal liqueur.

BETWEEN THE SHEETS

A delicious derivative of the Sidecar, usually attributed to Harry MacElhone of the famed Harry's New York Bar, Paris.

1 MEASURE COGNAC

1 MEASURE AGED RUM

1 MEASURE COINTREAU

¾ MEASURE LEMON JUICE

1 TSP SUGAR SYRUP

LEMON TWIST, TO GARNISH

Add all the ingredients to your cocktail shaker.
Shake vigorously and double strain into a chilled Martini glass.
Garnish with a twist of lemon.

BITTERS
Cocktail bitters are blends of distilled grain alcohols which are then infused with natural ingredients including herbs, spices, roots, tree barks and fruit peels. They can be used as a kind of cocktail seasoning whereby adding a few drops will provide an intense flavour boost, rather like certain oils or vinegars in cooking. The most commonly used cocktail bitters would be Angostura, Peychaud's and orange.

BLINKER

First recorded in 1934, the Blinker was something of a rarity for the time by using grapefruit juice as an ingredient. Spice from the rye and bitterness from the grapefruit are balanced by the fruity sweetness of grenadine.

2 MEASURES RYE WHISKEY

1 MEASURE PINK GRAPEFRUIT JUICE

½ MEASURE GRENADINE

LEMON TWIST, TO GARNISH

Add all the ingredients to your cocktail shaker.
Shake vigorously and double strain into a chilled coupette glass.
Garnish with a lemon twist.

BLOODY MARY

A Bloody Mary is quite rightly a wholly subjective drinking experience that varies from one person to another – the only staples being vodka and tomato juice. The recipe here is a useful starting point, but all seasoning and spicing can and should be adjusted to taste.

2 MEASURES VODKA

5 MEASURES TOMATO JUICE

½ MEASURE LEMON JUICE

4 DASHES WORCESTERSHIRE SAUCE

2 DASHES TABASCO SAUCE

1 TBSP HORSERADISH CREAM

PINCH OF SALT

PINCH OF CRACKED BLACK PEPPER

TO GARNISH

CELERY STICK

LEMON WEDGE

GREEN OLIVES

Add all the ingredients to a highball glass, stirring in cubed ice as you go.
Garnish with a celery stick, lemon wedge and green olives.

BLUE CURAÇAO

Blue Curaçao is simply orange Curaçao, which is distilled to have no colour, with a flavourless blue food colouring. Initially intended to give an exotic or mysterious feel, it is now seen and used in a rather tongue-in-cheek manner as a quirky, retro addition to cocktails.

BLUE HAWAIIAN

In essence, this is a Piña Colada turned blue – silly and delicious in equal measure.

2 MEASURES WHITE RUM
½ MEASURE BLUE CURAÇAO
1 MEASURE COCONUT CREAM
3 MEASURES PINEAPPLE JUICE
TO GARNISH
PINEAPPLE WEDGE
COCKTAIL CHERRY

Add all the ingredients to a food processor or blender and blend with a handful of cubed ice.
Pour into a hurricane glass and garnish with a pineapple wedge and a cocktail cherry.

Bobby Burns

A delicious variant of the Rob Roy cocktail, itself an interpretation of the Manhattan. A dash of Bénédictine brings herbal sweetness and depth of flavour.

2 MEASURES SCOTTISH WHISKY
1½ MEASURES SWEET VERMOUTH
¼ MEASURE BÉNÉDICTINE
2 DASHES ANGOSTURA BITTERS
LEMON TWIST, TO GARNISH

Add all the ingredients to a cocktail shaker or mixing glass, and fill with cubed ice. Stir for 30 seconds, and strain into a chilled coupette glass. Garnish with a lemon twist.

Bombay Punch
SERVES 20–30

A sumptuous, show-stopping celebratory punch. Balance and dilution are the key elements here.

1 BOTTLE COGNAC
1 BOTTLE FINO SHERRY
¼ BOTTLE MARASCHINO
¼ BOTTLE CURAÇAO
2 CUPS LEMON JUICE
1½ CUPS SUGAR SYRUP
2 BOTTLES CHILLED CHAMPAGNE

2 BOTTLES SODA WATER

TO GARNISH

ORANGE SLICES

LEMON SLICES

SEASONAL FRUIT

MINT SPRIGS

Add all the ingredients to a large punch bowl and fill with cubed ice.
Stir gently and garnish with slices of orange and lemon, seasonal fruit and mint.

BOULEVARDIER

Essentially a Negroni made with whiskey instead of gin, the original recipe dates back to Harry's New York Bar, Paris, in the 1920s. Simple, but utterly delicious.

1½ MEASURES BOURBON

1 MEASURE SWEET VERMOUTH

1 MEASURE CAMPARI

LEMON TWIST, TO GARNISH

Fill an old-fashioned glass with cubed ice, and add all the ingredients.
Stir for 10 seconds and garnish with a lemon twist.

BOURBON

Bourbon is a style of American whiskey. Known for its rich sweetness and notes of caramel and vanilla, it is often incorrectly stated that to be a bourbon it must be made in Kentucky. Bourbon can be made anywhere in America, so long as its cereal make-up, or "mash bill", contains at least 51% corn – the remaining ingredients being rye and malted barley.

BRAMBLE

Created by the late, great Dick Bradsell in the 1980s this Gin Sour flavoured with crème de mûre is a true modern classic. Sharp, fruity and boozy. Sensational.

2 MEASURES GIN

1 MEASURE LEMON JUICE

½ MEASURE SUGAR SYRUP

½ MEASURE CRÈME DE MÛRE

TO GARNISH

BLACKBERRIES

LEMON WEDGE

Fill an old-fashioned glass with crushed ice, packing it in tightly.
Add the gin, lemon juice and sugar syrup and stir briefly.
Slowly drizzle over the crème de mûre, so that it creates a "bleeding" effect down through the drink.
Top with more crushed ice and garnish with blackberries and a lemon wedge.

BRANDY ALEXANDER

As much a dessert as it is a cocktail. A luxurious after-dinner treat.

1½ MEASURES COGNAC

1½ MEASURES CRÈME DE CACAO

1 MEASURE DOUBLE CREAM

COCOA POWER, TO GARNISH

Add all the ingredients to the bottom half of your cocktail shaker, and half-fill the top piece with ice.
Shake vigorously and strain into a wine glass.
Garnish with a dusting of cocoa powder.

BRANDY CRUSTA

Created by Joseph Santini in New Orleans in the 1850s. The sugar frosting, or crust – hence the name – is essential to balance the intense sharpness of the ingredients.

1½ MEASURES COGNAC

½ MEASURE COINTREAU

½ MEASURE MARASCHINO

1 MEASURE LEMON JUICE

2 DASHES ANGOSTURA BITTERS

CASTER SUGAR, FOR FROSTING

ORANGE AND LEMON TWISTS, TO GARNISH

Add all the ingredients to your cocktail shaker.
Shake vigorously and strain into a sugar-frosted wine glass.
Garnish with twists of lemon and orange.

BREAKFAST MARTINI

Another modern classic, created in 1996 at the Lanesborough Hotel, London. The inspiration for Salvatore Calabrese's witty riff on the White Lady cocktail was said to have come to him at breakfast. Whether his breakfast also included gin is unclear…

1¾ MEASURES GIN

½ MEASURE COINTREAU

¾ MEASURE LEMON JUICE

1 TSP ORANGE MARMALADE

TO GARNISH

ORANGE TWIST

QUARTER OF TOAST

(OPTIONAL)

Add all the ingredients to your cocktail shaker and give the liquid a quick stir to break up the marmalade.
Shake vigorously and double strain into a chilled Martini glass.
Garnish with an orange twist and, if you wish, a small slice of toast.

BRITISH MOJITO

A spicier and more savoury alternative to the Cuban classic, while retaining a pleasant floral softness from elderflower. A summer garden in a glass.

2 MEASURES GIN

¾ MEASURE LIME JUICE

½ MEASURE ELDERFLOWER CORDIAL

6–8 MINT LEAVES

SODA WATER, TO TOP

TO GARNISH

LIME WEDGE

MINT SPRIG

Add all the ingredients
except the soda water to a
highball glass.
Fill the glass with crushed
ice, and churn with a bar
spoon.
Add a splash of soda water,
and top up with more
crushed ice.
Garnish with a lime wedge
and a mint sprig.

BRONX

*Originating in New York City
and first appearing in print in
1908, Bronx was a hugely
popular pre-Prohibition snifter.
In essence, it is simply a Gin
Manhattan freshened with a
splash of orange juice.
Delightful.*

2 MEASURES GIN

¼ MEASURE SWEET VERMOUTH

¼ MEASURE DRY VERMOUTH

1 MEASURE ORANGE JUICE

Add all the ingredients to
your cocktail shaker.
Shake vigorously with cubed

ice and double strain into
a chilled coupette glass.
No garnish.

BUCKS FIZZ

*Said to be created in 1921 at
the Buck's Club in London. As
popular today as ever, the key
to this simple aperitif is using
freshly squeezed orange juice.*

2 MEASURES CHILLED FRESH
ORANGE JUICE

4 MEASURES CHILLED
CHAMPAGNE

Add half the Champagne
to a Champagne flute, then
carefully add the orange
juice and the rest of the
Champagne.

> *"With all respect to James Bond, a Martini should be stirred, not shaken."*
>
> Kingsley Amis, *Everyday Drinking*

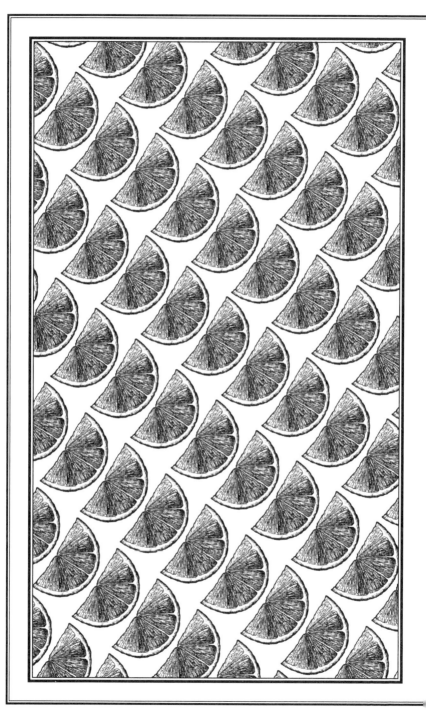

C

CAEN CAEN

CAIPIRINHA

CAIRPRIOSKA

CAMOMILE COLLINS

CANADIAN DAISY

CHAMPAGNE JULEP

CHAMPS-ÉLYSÉES

CLASSIC CHAMPAGNE COCKTAIL

CLOVER CLUB

COBBLER

COCONUT DAIQUIRI

COGNAC

COMBINED FORCES

CORPSE REVIVER NO 2

COSMOPOLITAN

CUCUMBER COOLER

Caen Caen

A Manhattan by way of France. Fruited, sharp and sweet, this makes for a fabulous digestive.

2 MEASURES COGNAC

1 MEASURE CALVADOS

½ MEASURE SWEET VERMOUTH

LEMON TWIST, TO GARNISH

Add all the ingredients to a cocktail shaker or mixing glass, and fill with cubed ice. Stir for 30 seconds, and strain into a chilled Martini glass. Garnish with a lemon twist.

Caipirinha

Translated literally, Caipirinha means "little country girl" and – as with so many traditional cocktails – was conceived originally to soften and smooth cachaça's naturally rough edges. The key is achieving the wonderful crunch of sugar, without the result being overly cloying. Short, sweet and deadly.

2 MEASURES CACHAÇA

8 LIME WEDGES, PLUS AN EXTRA WEDGE TO GARNISH

2 TSP CASTER SUGAR

Add the lime wedges and sugar to the bottom of a rocks glass and muddle together.
Pour in the cachaça, fill the glass with crushed ice and churn vigorously.
Top with more ice and garnish with a lime wedge.

CAIPRIOSKA

Europe's answer to the Caipirinha, though closer to a Vodka Sour on the rocks in style.

2 MEASURES VODKA

1 MEASURE LIME JUICE

¾ MEASURE SUGAR SYRUP

LIME WEDGE, TO GARNISH

Fill a rocks glass with crushed ice, add all the ingredients and churn vigorously.
Top with more crushed ice and garnish with a lime wedge.

CAMOMILE COLLINS

A delicate alternative to a Tom Collins.

2 MEASURES GIN

1 MEASURE LEMON JUICE

¾ MEASURE SUGAR SYRUP

SODA WATER, TO TOP

1 CAMOMILE TEA BAG

LEMON WEDGE, TO GARNISH

Pour the gin into a highball glass, then add the camomile tea bag.
Leave for 5 minutes.
Remove the tea bag, fill the glass with cubed ice and gently add in the remaining ingredients, stirring as you go.
Garnish with a lemon wedge.

CANADIAN DAISY

The "Daisy" category of cocktails can be loosely defined as being a Sour that is lengthened with soda water. This is a refreshing Whisky Highball, sweetened with raspberry. Highly drinkable.

2 MEASURES CANADIAN RYE WHISKY

¾ MEASURE LEMON JUICE

2 TSP RASPBERRY SYRUP

2 TSP SUGAR SYRUP

SODA WATER, TO TOP

RASPBERRIES, TO GARNISH

Fill a coupette glass with cubed ice, and add all the ingredients except the soda water.
Stir gently for a few seconds and top up with soda water. Garnish with raspberries.

CHAMPAGNE JULEP

An impressive tipple for a garden party. Here we have used Cognac but bourbon, rye or rum would substitute just as well. Luxury in a glass.

1 MEASURE COGNAC

1 TSP SUGAR

8 MINT LEAVES

CHAMPAGNE, TO TOP

MINT SPRIGS, TO GARNISH

Add the Cognac, sugar and mint leaves to a highball glass filled with crushed ice and churn.
Top with Champagne and more crushed ice and garnish with mint sprigs.

CHAMPS-ÉLYSÉES

A powerful and aromatic speakeasy-style Sidecar variation, the earliest reference to it appearing in "The Savoy Cocktail Book" (1930).

1½ MEASURES COGNAC

½ MEASURE YELLOW
CHARTREUSE

¾ MEASURE LEMON JUICE

½ MEASURE SUGAR SYRUP

2 DASHES ANGOSTURA BITTERS

LEMON TWIST, TO GARNISH

Add all the ingredients to
your cocktail shaker, shake
vigorously and double strain
into a chilled coupette glass.
Garnish with a lemon twist.

1 MEASURE COGNAC

1 SUGAR CUBE

3–4 DASHES ANGOSTURA
BITTERS

CHILLED CHAMPAGNE, TO TOP

LEMON TWIST, TO FINISH

On a clean surface, coat the
sugar cube in the Angostura
bitters then drop it into a
Champagne flute.
Add the Cognac and gently
top with Champagne.
To finish, spray the oils of a
lemon twist over the top of
the drink, then discard it.

CLASSIC
CHAMPAGNE
COCKTAIL

*The marvel of the Classic
Champagne Cocktail is how the
drink changes with time. It
sweetens as the sugar cube
dissolves, while intensifying the
Champagne's carbonation. A
timeless, elegant celebration.*

CLOVER CLUB

*A pre-Prohibition Gin Sour
enlivened by raspberries. Named
after the gentlemen's club where
it was first created in the 1800s.*

2 MEASURES GIN

¾ MEASURE LEMON JUICE

¾ MEASURE SUGAR SYRUP

5 RASPBERRIES, PLUS EXTRA TO
GARNISH

½ MEASURE EGG WHITE

Add all the ingredients to your cocktail shaker and vigorously "dry shake" without ice for 10 seconds. Take the shaker apart, add cubed ice and shake vigorously.
Strain into a coupette glass and garnish with raspberries.

1 MEASURE WHITE RUM

1 MEASURE COCONUT RUM

1 MEASURE LIME JUICE

¾ MEASURE SUGAR SYRUP

LIME WHEEL, TO GARNISH

Add all the ingredients to your cocktail shaker.
Shake vigorously and double strain into a chilled coupette glass.
Garnish with a lime wheel on the edge of the glass.

COBBLER

A "cobbler" is an old-style American cocktail dating back to the 1820s. Sugar, citrus and a base spirit or liqueur are shaken and then poured over crushed ice, or what were then known as "cobbles". By far the most popular and widely drank version at the time was the Sherry Cobbler, which remains a well-loved classic to this day.

COCONUT DAIQUIRI

An easy coconut twist on the classic Daiquiri. Fresh and tropical.

COGNAC

Cognac is the name given to brandy that has, since the 17th century, been produced in the town and surrounding area of Cognac in France. It is widely considered to be the finest of all spirits, and is distilled from a selection of wine grape varieties which are unsuitable for wine making because of their acidity. By law, Cognac must be aged for an absolute minimum of two years in French oak barrels, though it will usually be aged for far longer.

COMBINED FORCES

An elegant Vodka Martini. A fantastic alternative to gin as a pre-dinner aperitif.

2 MEASURES VODKA

½ MEASURE TRIPLE SEC

½ MEASURE DRY VERMOUTH

2 DASHES ORANGE BITTERS

LEMON TWIST, TO GARNISH

Add all the ingredients to your cocktail shaker or mixing glass, and fill with cubed ice.
Stir for 30 seconds, and strain into a chilled Martini glass. Garnish with a twist of lemon.

CORPSE REVIVER No. 2

According to its creator Harry Craddock in "The Savoy Cocktail Book" (1930), "four of these taken in quick succession will unrevive the corpse again." Floral, aromatic and bracing flavours combine to make this a bartender's favourite the world over.

1 MEASURE GIN

1 MEASURE LEMON JUICE

1 MEASURE LILLET BLANC

1 MEASURE COINTREAU

2 DROPS ABSINTHE

LEMON TWIST, TO GARNISH

Add all the ingredients to your cocktail shaker.
Shake vigorously with cubed ice and double strain into a chilled coupette glass.
Garnish with a lemon twist.

COSMOPOLITAN

Immortalized in the late 1990s by the television show "Sex in the City", its cultural significance possibly outweighs its quality. However, the popularity of the Cosmopolitan shows little sign of waning. Its origins have been hotly disputed since the 1970s, and the version below reflects the best of them all.

1½ MEASURES VODKA

¾ MEASURE COINTREAU

½ MEASURE LIME JUICE

1½ MEASURES CRANBERRY JUICE

FLAMED ORANGE TWIST, TO GARNISH

Add all the ingredients to your cocktail shaker.
Shake vigorously with cubed ice and double strain into a chilled Martini glass.
Garnish with a flamed orange twist.

CUCUMBER COOLER

A Mojito-alternative for gin lovers. Cucumber brings a welcome freshness to this pleasant summer sipper.

2 MEASURES GIN

½ MEASURE SUGAR SYRUP

½ MEASURE LEMON JUICE

5 CUBES CUCUMBER

6 MINT LEAVES

SODA WATER, TO TOP

TO GARNISH

CUCUMBER SLICES

MINT SPRIG

Add all the ingredients except the soda water to a highball glass and muddle.
Fill the glass with crushed ice and churn.
Top with soda water, and garnish with cucumber slices and a sprig of mint.

"With alcoholic ritual, the whole point is generosity. If you open a bottle of wine, for heaven's sake have the grace to throw away the damn cork."

Christopher Hitchens, *Everyday Drinking*

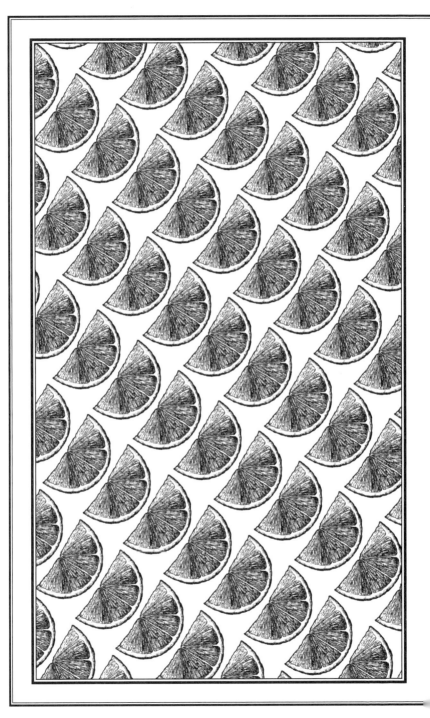

D

DAIQUIRI

Supposedly created by an American mining engineer working in Cuba in 1898, the Daiquiri is in essence a Sour made with rum. In reality, it now represents an entire category of drinks. A thing of great beauty – sharp and invigorating.

2 MEASURES LIGHT RUM

1 MEASURE LIME JUICE

¾ MEASURE SUGAR SYRUP

Add all the ingredients to your cocktail shaker. Shake vigorously with cubed ice and double strain into a chilled coupette glass. No garnish.

DEATH IN THE AFTERNOON

A favourite of Ernest Hemingway apparently, though to suggest Hemingway had a favourite anything when it came to drinking possibly belies his zeal for the pastime. Approach with caution.

½ MEASURE ABSINTHE

CHILLED CHAMPAGNE, TO TOP

Pour the absinthe into the bottom of a Champagne flute, then slowly and carefully top with the chilled Champagne.
No garnish.

DELFT DONKEY

A sweetly spiced Gin Highball, or grown-up ginger beer…

2 MEASURES GIN

1 MEASURE LEMON JUICE

GINGER BEER, TO TOP

LEMON WEDGE, TO GARNISH

Add all the ingredients to a highball glass filled with cubed ice and garnish with a lemon wedge.

DESERT DAISY

Sharp and fruity, a Tequila Mojito of sorts. Strawberries and tequila make for an unexpected and surprisingly pleasant combination.

1½ MEASURES TEQUILA

½ MEASURE STRAWBERRY LIQUEUR

1 MEASURE LIME JUICE

½ MEASURE SUGAR SYRUP

TO GARNISH

LIME WEDGE

STRAWBERRY HALF

Add the tequila, lime juice and sugar syrup to an old-fashioned glass filled with crushed ice.
Churn, and then float the strawberry liqueur over the top.
Top with more crushed ice, and garnish with a lime wedge and a strawberry half.

DIRTY MARTINI

An apparent creation of none other than President Franklin Delano Roosevelt – the dry saltiness of the Dirty Martini is loathed and loved in equal measure, depending on the individual drinker's feelings about olives. Delicious. Or awful.

2½ MEASURES VODKA

¼ MEASURE DRY VERMOUTH

½ MEASURE OLIVE BRINE

OLIVES, TO GARNISH

Add all the ingredients to a cocktail shaker or mixing glass, and fill with cubed ice. Stir for 30 seconds, and strain into a chilled Martini glass. Garnish with olives.

DISTILLATION
Nearly all spirits go through the process of distillation, as do perfumes and many herbal medicines, whereby impurities and unwanted chemical compounds are removed by the processes of boiling, evaporation and condensation. Each product will have its own idiosyncratic process, but the principle will remain the same. A trip to a spirit distillery of any sort will be a day very well spent.

DOOBS MARTINI

An excellent Martini alternative, with powerful notes of sour hedgerow fruit.

1¾ MEASURES GIN

1 MEASURE SLOE GIN

¾ MEASURE DRY VERMOUTH

4 DASHES ORANGE BITTERS

ORANGE TWIST, TO GARNISH

Add all the ingredients to a cocktail shaker or mixing glass, and fill with cubed ice. Stir for 30 seconds, and strain into a chilled Martini glass. Garnish with an orange twist.

DRY DAIQUIRI

A superb modern Daiquiri variant created by noted London bartender Kevin Armstrong. The subtle additions of passion fruit and Campari bring astringency and dry complexity to the classic Daiquiri. An absolute must-try.

2 MEASURES LIGHT RUM

¾ MEASURE LIME JUICE

½ MEASURE SUGAR SYRUP

2 TSP PASSION FRUIT SYRUP

2 TSP CAMPARI

ORANGE TWIST, TO GARNISH

Add all the ingredients to your cocktail shaker.
Shake vigorously and double strain into a chilled coupette glass.
Garnish with an orange twist.

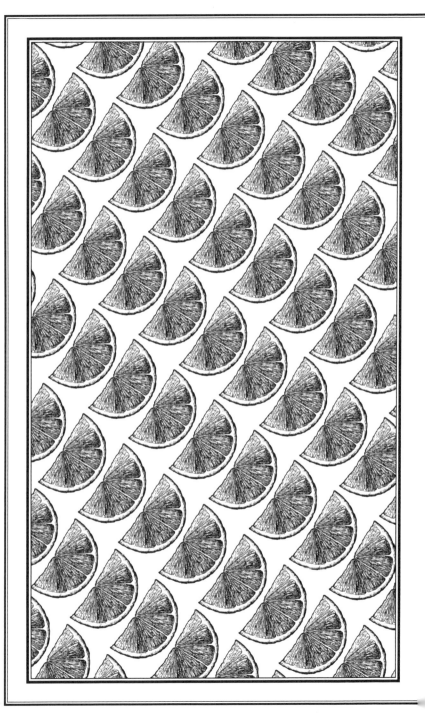

E

EARL'S PUNCH
MAKES 1 JUG

A light and approachable sharing punch that can be assembled in moments. Fresh bergamot from the Earl Grey and sour-sweet pink grapefruit combine wonderfully.

4 MEASURES GIN

6 MEASURES COLD EARL GREY TEA

6 MEASURES GRAPEFRUIT JUICE

5 MEASURES SUGAR SYRUP

SODA WATER, TO TOP

TO GARNISH

PINK GRAPEFRUIT SLICES

ROSEMARY SPRIGS

Fill a jug with cubed ice and add all the ingredients except the soda water.
Stir well, then top with soda water and garnish with slices of grapefruit and some rosemary sprigs.
Serve in wine glasses.

EAST SIDE COCKTAIL

A refreshing cucumber twist on the classic Southside Cocktail. This is an excellent introduction to classic cocktail-making for gin lovers.

2 MEASURES GIN

1 MEASURE LIME JUICE

¾ MEASURE SUGAR SYRUP

3 CUBES CUCUMBER

6 MINT LEAVES

THIN CUCUMBER SLICE, TO GARNISH

Muddle the cucumber and mint in the bottom of your cocktail shaker, then add the remaining ingredients. Shake and double strain into a chilled coupette glass. Garnish with thin slice of cucumber.

EGG NOG

There are countless ways to assemble this Christmas favourite. Here is a simple and delicious cold version. It would do just as well by being gently heated, or by using Cognac instead of rum.

2 MEASURES AGED RUM

¾ MEASURE SUGAR SYRUP

1 EGG

3 MEASURES WHOLE MILK

3 MEASURES SINGLE CREAM

TO GARNISH

CINNAMON STICK

GROUND NUTMEG

Add all the ingredients to your cocktail shaker. Shake vigorously and strain into a chilled wine glass filled with cubed ice. Garnish with a cinnamon stick and dusting of ground nutmeg.

EL DIABLO

A fruity Mule variation. Perfect for those occasions when only tequila will do.

1½ MEASURES GOLD TEQUILA
½ MEASURE CRÈME DE CASSIS
¾ MEASURE LIME JUICE
GINGER ALE, TO TOP
LIME WHEEL, TO GARNISH

Fill a highball glass with ice and add the tequila, crème de cassis and lime juice.
Stir briefly, then top up with ginger ale.
Garnish with a lime wheel.

ENGLISH GARDEN FIZZ

A gentle Gin Fizz with flavours of the English orchard. Crowd pleasing and sessionable.

2 MEASURES GIN
2 MEASURES APPLE JUICE
¾ MEASURE LEMON JUICE
½ MEASURE ELDERFLOWER
CORDIAL
SODA WATER, TO TOP
TO GARNISH
CUCUMBER SLICES
LEMON SLICES

Add all the ingredients except the soda water to your cocktail shaker and shake briefly.
Strain the contents into a highball glass filled with cubed ice, top up with the soda water and garnish with slices of cucumber and lemon.

ESPRESSO MARTINI

Another modern classic from London's Dick Bradsell, when asked by a customer for drink that would "wake me up, and f*ck me up." The key here is technique. For the desired foam, you must shake vigorously for a good 10 seconds, and ensure your coffee is of the best quality available.

1½ MEASURES VODKA

1 MEASURE COFFEE LIQUEUR

1 MEASURE FRESH ESPRESSO
COFFEE

½ MEASURE SUGAR SYRUP

3 COFFEE BEANS, TO GARNISH

Add all the ingredients to
your cocktail shaker.
Shake vigorously and double
strain into a chilled Martini
glass.
Garnish with the coffee
beans.

6 DROPS ABSINTHE

CHILLED ROSÉ CHAMPAGNE, TO
TOP

Rinse a Champagne flute
with the absinthe, by
dropping it in and swilling it
around.
Shake the glass clean,
discarding any remaining
liquid, then add the rest of
the ingredients.

EVE

*An elegant Champagne aperitif.
Merely a "sense" of the absinthe
is what we want, giving a subtle
but vibrant flavour contrast.*

½ MEASURE COGNAC

2 TSP COINTREAU

2 TSP SUGAR SYRUP

F

FINO HIGHBALL

FISH HOUSE PUNCH

FIX

FLORA DORA

FOG CUTTER

FRENCH 75

FRENCH KISS

FRENCH MARTINI

FINO HIGHBALL

A Gin and Tonic may at first seem a quintessentially English idea, but it is in Spain that the drink has been elevated to true greatness. Dry, crisp and bright, with a satisfactory bitterness coming from the tonic – this is a Highball for those looking for something different.

1 MEASURE GIN

1 MEASURE FINO SHERRY

½ MEASURE LEMON JUICE

2 TSP SUGAR SYRUP

1 MEASURE ORANGE JUICE

TONIC WATER, TO TOP

LEMON WEDGE, TO GARNISH

Add all the ingredients except the tonic water to your cocktail shaker. Shake, and then pour into a highball glass filled with cubed ice. Top with tonic water and garnish with a lemon wedge.

FISH HOUSE PUNCH

A traditional punch dating back to 18th-century North America, and reported to be a favourite of George Washington. Rich and well balanced, this could easily be scaled up to be served in a punch bowl at a party.

1 MEASURE COGNAC

1 MEASURE RUM

½ MEASURE PEACH LIQUEUR

1 MEASURE LEMON JUICE

½ MEASURE SUGAR SYRUP

2 MEASURES COLD ENGLISH BREAKFAST TEA

SODA WATER, TO TOP

LEMON WEDGE, TO GARNISH

Add all ingredients except the soda water to your cocktail shaker and shake vigorously.
Strain into a wine or rocks glass filled with cubed ice, top with soda water and garnish with a lemon wedge.

FIX

The simplest of Sours, and really the very building blocks of all drinks making – first recorded in Jerry Thomas's "How to Mix Drinks" (1862). Gin can easily be substituted for a different spirit.

2 MEASURES GIN

1 MEASURE LEMON

¾ MEASURE SUGAR SYRUP

SEASONAL FRUIT, TO GARNISH

Add the ingredients to a rocks glass filled with crushed ice.
Churn, and garnish with seasonal fruit of your choosing.

FLORA DORA

A fruited Gin Mule, dating back to the 19th century and popular in high society. Effervescent and very pretty.

2 MEASURES GIN

1 MEASURE LIME JUICE

¾ MEASURE RASPBERRY
LIQUEUR

GINGER ALE, TO TOP

TO GARNISH

RASPBERRY

LIME WEDGE

Shake the first three ingredients and strain into a highball glass filled with cubed ice, top with ginger ale and garnish with a raspberry and a wedge of lime.

½ MEASURE SHERRY

½ MEASURE ORGEAT

¾ MEASURE LEMON JUICE

2 MEASURES ORANGE JUICE

ORANGE SLICE, TO GARNISH

Add all the ingredients to your cocktail shaker, shake and strain into an old-fashioned glass filled with cubed ice.
Garnish with an orange slice.

FOG CUTTER

Richly flavoured and wickedly strong, this complex rum punch is a Tiki classic. Its origins are as foggy as its name suggests but what is certain is that too many of them will have you on the floor. Quaff carefully.

1 MEASURE LIGHT RUM

1 MEASURE COGNAC

½ MEASURE GIN

FRENCH 75

Also, but less popularly, called a 75 Cocktail, this drink dates back to Harry's New York Bar in Paris, created in 1915, this is as much a Tom Collins with a Champagne top as it is anything else. Dangerously drinkable.

1 MEASURE GIN

½ MEASURE LEMON JUICE

½ MEASURE SUGAR SYRUP

CHILLED CHAMPAGNE, TO TOP

LEMON TWIST, TO GARNISH

Shake the gin, lemon juice and sugar syrup vigorously and strain into a Champagne flute.
Top with Champagne and garnish with a lemon twist.

FRENCH KISS

A Negroni of sorts, with the wine notes of Dubonnet and dry vermouth bringing an approachable softness.

1 MEASURE GIN

1 MEASURE DUBONNET

1 MEASURE DRY VERMOUTH

LEMON TWIST, TO GARNISH

Add of the ingredients to a rocks glass filled with cubed ice.
Stir briefly and garnish with a lemon twist.

FRENCH MARTINI

A crowd-pleasing modern classic, the French Martini is just frivolous enough to be taken seriously.

1½ MEASURES VODKA

1 MEASURE CHAMBORD

2 MEASURES PINEAPPLE JUICE

RASPBERRIES, TO GARNISH

Add all the ingredients to your cocktail shaker, shake vigorously and strain into a chilled coupette glass.
Garnish with raspberries.

G

G AND TEA

A peach iced tea, spiked with gin. The savoury depth of the rosemary garnish creates a wonderful contrast between aroma and taste.

1½ MEASURES GIN

¾ MEASURE PEACH LIQUEUR

¾ MEASURE LEMON JUICE

½ MEASURE SUGAR SYRUP

2 MEASURES COLD ENGLISH

BREAKFAST TEA

TO GARNISH

LEMON WEDGE

ROSEMARY SPRIG

Add all the ingredients to your cocktail shaker, shake vigorously and strain into a chilled highball glass filled with cubed ice.
Garnish with a lemon wedge and a sprig of rosemary.

GENEVER

Genever is the traditional Dutch liquor from which gin was derived. It was initially a distillation of malt wine infused with herbs and spices, the most predominant being juniper, or genever. Over time, and as production methods improved, two dominant styles emerged, those of Oude (Young) Genever and Jonge (Young) Genever – the differences in them referring to the cereals that went into their respective blends, as opposed to aging.

GEORGIA JULEP

A rich and fruity Julep variation – with a nod to its local produce and colonial past. To be sipped with friends on a summer evening.

2 MEASURES COGNAC

½ MEASURE PEACH LIQUEUR

2 TSP SUGAR SYRUP

2 DASHES ANGOSTURA BITTERS

6–8 MINT LEAVES

MINT SPRIG, TO GARNISH

Add all the ingredients to an old-fashioned glass and stir. Fill with crushed ice and churn for 10 seconds. Top with more crushed ice and garnish with a sprig of mint.

GIBSON MARTINI

A classic Gin Martini, differentiated by using a picante onion garnish rather than an olive or lemon twist – which gives a pleasingly unusual acidity. As with all stirred classics, dilution and temperature will be your most important variables to control. Divine.

2½ MEASURES GIN

½ MEASURE DRY VERMOUTH

COCKTAIL ONIONS, TO

GARNISH

Add the gin and dry vermouth to a cocktail shaker or mixing glass, and fill with cubed ice.
Stir for 30 seconds, and strain into a chilled Martini glass. Garnish generously with cocktail onions.

GIMLET

The recipe for the Gimlet has evolved with time, and varies from source to source, with some calling for just lime cordial, others for fresh lime and a touch of sugar syrup. However, the result will remain consistent – sweet, sharp and strong.

2½ MEASURES GIN
½ MEASURE LIME CORDIAL
½ MEASURE LIME JUICE
LIME TWIST, TO GARNISH

Add all the ingredients to your cocktail shaker, shake vigorously and strain into a chilled coupette glass. Garnish with a lime twist.

GIN

Gin as we know it today is a grain spirit flavoured with botanicals, most notably juniper, and originating in Holland in the 1500s as "Genever". Gin production in a crude sense had existed in Britain for a similar amount of time, but by pioneering the process of continuous distillation, the Victorians created the subtler, more complex and far safer London Dry Gin which is enjoyed with as much enthusiasm today as ever before.

GIN FIZZ

The classic Gin Fizz (or Silver Fizz) should be sweet, sour and fluffy as a cloud. Feel free to experiment with different base spirits; most will work wonderfully.

2 MEASURES GIN

1 MEASURE LEMON JUICE

¾ MEASURE SUGAR SYRUP

½ MEASURE EGG WHITE

SODA WATER, TO TOP

Add all the ingredients
except the soda water to
your cocktail shaker and
vigorously "dry shake"
without ice for 10 seconds.
Take the shaker apart,
add cubed ice and shake
vigorously.
Strain into a chilled highball
glass and top with soda
water.
No ice, no garnish.

GINGER SNAP

*A Whisky Mac for vodka lovers,
and as snappy as its name
suggests.*

2 MEASURES VODKA

1 MEASURE GINGER WINE

ORANGE SLICE, TO GARNISH

Add the ingredients to a
rocks glass filled with cubed
ice and stir gently.

Garnish with a slice of
orange.

GODFATHER

*A simple yet delicious snifter for
whisky lovers. Amaretto's sweet
almond flavour complements the
heather honey smoothness of
Scottish whisky.*

2 MEASURES SCOTTISH WHISKY

1 MEASURE AMARETTO

Add both ingredients to a
rocks glass filled with ice and
stir.
No garnish.

GOLDEN
CADILLAC

*A sweet and luxurious dessert
cocktail, this is a refined Piña
Colada of sorts; 1970s New York
in a glass and a true disco
classic.*

1½ MEASURES WHITE CRÈME DE CACAO

1½ MEASURES GALLIANO

1 MEASURE DOUBLE CREAM

GRATED NUTMEG, TO GARNISH

Add all the ingredients to a blender or food processor and blend with 7 cubes of ice.
Pour into a chilled wine glass and garnish with a dusting of grated nutmeg.

GOLDEN SOUR

A bright and elegant Scotch Sour, with warm notes of orange from the Cointreau.

2 MEASURES SCOTTISH WHISKY

½ MEASURE COINTREAU

1 MEASURE LEMON JUICE

½ MEASURE SUGAR SYRUP

LEMON WEDGE, TO GARNISH

Add all the ingredients to your cocktail shaker, shake vigorously and strain into a chilled coupette glass.
Garnish with a lemon wedge.

GORGEOUS GRACE

A delightful Champagne aperitif. This is a miniature Sidecar charged with bubbles – perfectly balanced decadence.

1 MEASURE COGNAC

½ MEASURE COINTREAU

½ MEASURE LEMON JUICE

1 TSP SUGAR SYRUP

CHILLED CHAMPAGNE, TO TOP

ORANGE TWIST, TO GARNISH

Vigorously shake the Cognac, Cointreau, lemon juice and sugar syrup and strain into a Champagne flute.
Top with Champagne and garnish with an orange twist.

GRAPPA MANHATTAN

An Italian Manhattan. Grappa's rougher wine notes make this a highly drinkable digestive.

2 MEASURES GRAPPA

1 MEASURE SWEET VERMOUTH

½ MEASURE MARASCHINO

2 DASHES ANGOSTURA BITTERS

GREEN OLIVES, TO GARNISH

Add all the ingredients to
a cocktail shaker or mixing
glass, and fill with cubed ice.
Stir for 30 seconds, and strain
into a chilled Martini glass.
Garnish with olives.

1 MEASURE SINGLE CREAM

1 MEASURE MILK

MINT LEAF, TO GARNISH

Add all the ingredients to
your cocktail shaker, shake
vigorously and strain into a
chilled coupette glass.
Garnish with a mint leaf.

GRASSHOPPER

*A mint-choc dessert cocktail.
Wildly popular in the 1970s
and originating from New
Orleans; try adding a measure
of Cognac for an even richer
after-dinner treat.*

1½ MEASURES WHITE CRÈME DE
CACAO

1½ MEASURES CRÈME DE
MENTHE

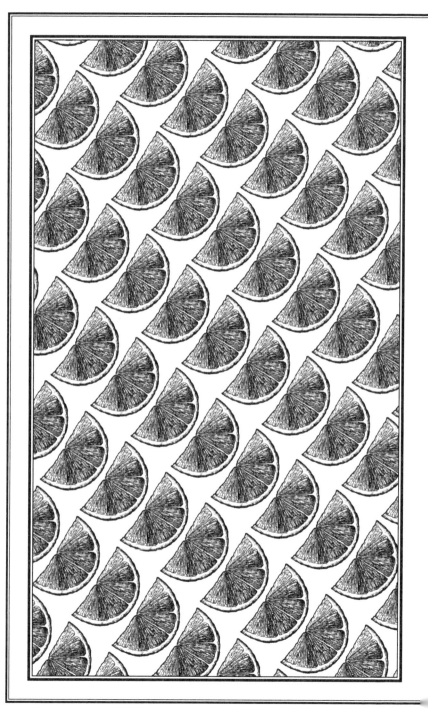

H

HAITI PUNCH

HANKY PANKY

HARLEQUIN

HARRY CRADDOCK

HARRY'S NEW YORK BAR, PARIS

HARVARD COCKTAIL

HARVEY WALLBANGER

HEDGEROW COLLINS

HEMINGWAY DAIQUIRI

HONEYDEW

HONG KONG SLING

HONOLULU

HURRICANE

HAITI PUNCH
SERVES 15

A tropical punch, made in the traditional style. Simple to assemble, complex and fruity.

½ BOTTLE COGNAC

½ BOTTLE ORANGE CURAÇAO

2 BOTTLES CHILLED SPARKLING
WINE

1 PINEAPPLE

TO GARNISH:

ORANGE SLICES

LEMON SLICES

PINEAPPLE LEAVES

Chop the pineapple, removing the skin if you like, and place the segments in a large punch bowl.
Fill the bowl with cubed ice, then carefully pour in the Cognac, Curaçao and sparkling wine.
Stir well, and garnish with slices of orange and lemon and pineapple leaves.
Serve in wine glasses.

HANKY PANKY

A subtle twist on the Martinez cocktail, created by Ada Coleman at the Savoy Hotel, London, in the early 1900s. Fernet Branca is an intensely bitter Italian amaro, and cuts through the sweetness of the vermouth superbly. Worth a try.

2 MEASURES GIN
1 MEASURE SWEET VERMOUTH
1 TBSP FERNET BRANCA
ORANGE TWIST, TO GARNISH

Add all the ingredients to a cocktail shaker or mixing glass, and fill with cubed ice. Stir for 30 seconds, and strain into a chilled Martini glass. Garnish with an orange twist.

HARLEQUIN

A fruity and sharp Fizz with apricots and cherries. Refreshing and invigorating.

1 MEASURE KIRSCH
1 MEASURE APRICOT BRANDY
2 MEASURES ORANGE JUICE
½ MEASURE LEMON JUICE
½ MEASURE SUGAR SYRUP
SODA WATER, TO TOP
TO GARNISH
ORANGE SLICES
COCKTAIL CHERRY

Add all the ingredients except the soda water to your cocktail shaker and shake vigorously.
Strain into a rocks glass filled with cubed ice and top with soda water.
Garnish with slices of orange and a cocktail cherry.

HARRY CRADDOCK
Harry Craddock (1876 –1963) was an English bartender of global fame, garnered most notably from his tenure as head bartender of the American Bar of the Savoy Hotel, London, in the 1920s and 30s. A forefather of modern bartending, dozens of his recipes are still imbibed to this day. In 1930

he published "The Savoy Cocktail Book", arguably the most important cocktail book of the 20th century.

HARRY'S NEW YORK BAR, PARIS

Originally a bar for American ex-pats in Paris named simply the "New York Bar", and run by Scotsman Harry MacElhone, who eventually bought and renamed it "Harry's New York Bar" in 1923. Patronized by tourists, servicemen and celebrities alike, countless MacElhone creations are still drunk today as classics. His family still run the bar to this day, in the same spot at 5 Rue Daunou, where it has stood since 1911.

HARVARD COCKTAIL

A lively Cognac aperitif, said to predate the Manhattan cocktail. The soda water softens through the richness of the Cognac, creating a pleasing dryness.

2 MEASURES COGNAC

1 MEASURE SWEET VERMOUTH

2 DASHES ANGOSTURA BITTERS

1 MEASURE SODA WATER

ORANGE TWIST, TO GARNISH

Add all the ingredients to a cocktail shaker or mixing glass, and fill with cubed ice. Stir for 30 seconds, and strain into a chilled coupette glass. Top with the soda water and garnish with an orange twist.

HARVEY WALLBANGER

Probably known more for its name than its ingredients, the Harvey Wallbanger is something of a forgotten jewel of the 1970s.

Ensure you make it with freshly squeezed orange juice.

1½ MEASURES VODKA
½ MEASURE GALLIANO
5 MEASURES FRESH ORANGE JUICE
ORANGE SLICE, TO GARNISH

Add the vodka and orange juice to a hurricane or highball glass filled with ice. Stir, and then float the Galliano over the top. Garnish with a slice of orange.

½ MEASURE SUGAR SYRUP
SODA WATER, TO TOP

TO GARNISH
LEMON WEDGE
BLACKBERRY

Add all the ingredients except the soda water to a highball glass filled with cubed ice.
Stir gently, top with soda and garnish with a lemon wedge and a blackberry.

HEDGEROW COLLINS

Autumnal in feel, this is a deftly balanced Gin Highball with the faintest waft of Campari cutting through the rich sweetness of hedgerow fruit.

1½ MEASURES GIN
½ MEASURE CRÈME DE MÛRE
1 TSP CAMPARI
¾ MEASURE LEMON JUICE

HEMINGWAY DAIQUIRI

Created at Floridita in Havana for erstwhile barfly Ernest Hemingway, whose penchant for Daiquiris was only inhibited by his usually sour palate. Though superb, the Hemingway (or Papa Doble) is very sour, so add a touch more sugar if you wish.

1¾ MEASURES LIGHT RUM

¾ MEASURE MARASCHINO

1 MEASURE LIME JUICE

1 MEASURE GRAPEFRUIT JUICE

2 TSP SUGAR SYRUP

LIME WEDGE, TO GARNISH

Add all the ingredients to your cocktail shaker, shake vigorously and double strain into a chilled coupette glass. Garnish with a lime wedge on the side of the glass.

HONEYDEW

A crisply fruited Gin Frappé, topped with sparkling wine and with a welcome spike of anise. In many respects, the perfect drink.

1 MEASURE GIN

½ MEASURE LEMON JUICE

½ MEASURE SUGAR SYRUP

2 DROPS ABSINTHE OR PERNOD

5 CUBES HONEYDEW MELON

CHILLED PROSECCO, TO TOP

TO GARNISH

LEMON TWIST

ROSEMARY SPRIG

Add all the ingredients except the Prosecco to a blender or food processor and blend with 5 cubes of ice.
Pour into a chilled wine glass, top with Prosecco and garnish with a lemon twist and sprig of rosemary.

HONG KONG SLING

A floral riff on the Singapore Sling. Perfect for gin lovers with a sweet tooth.

2 MEASURES GIN

2 MEASURES LYCHEE JUICE

¾ MEASURE LEMON JUICE

½ MEASURE SUGAR SYRUP

SODA WATER, TO TOP

UNPEELED WHOLE LYCHEES, TO GARNISH

Add all the ingredients except the soda water to your cocktail shaker, shake vigorously and double strain into a hurricane glass filled with cubed ice.

Top with soda water and garnish with whole lychees.

HONOLULU

A fruity highball in the style of a Tiki punch, the dryness of the gin really cuts though the tropical sweetness.

2 MEASURES GIN

¾ MEASURE LEMON JUICE

½ MEASURE GRENADINE

1 MEASURE ORANGE JUICE

3 MEASURES PINEAPPLE JUICE

TO GARNISH

PINEAPPLE WEDGE

COCKTAIL CHERRY

Add all the ingredients to your cocktail shaker, shake vigorously and strain into a hurricane glass.
Garnish with a pineapple wedge and a cocktail cherry.

HURRICANE

Strong and sweet, and immortalized at Pat O'Brien's bar in New Orleans, most likely in the 1940s. This is a classic tropical punch variation, with rich fruit combining with sharp citrus and a heavy dose of different rums to create an ever so more-ish party classic; and such was its popularity, it even has a glass named after it.

1½ MEASURES WHITE RUM

1½ MEASURES DARK RUM

1 MEASURE LIME JUICE

¾ MEASURE PASSION FRUIT SYRUP

2 TSP GRENADINE

½ MEASURE ORANGE JUICE

½ MEASURE PINEAPPLE JUICE

TO GARNISH

ORANGE SLICE

COCKTAIL CHERRY

Add all the ingredients to your cocktail shaker, shake vigorously and strain into a hurricane glass filled with cubed ice.
Garnish with an orange slice and a cocktail cherry.

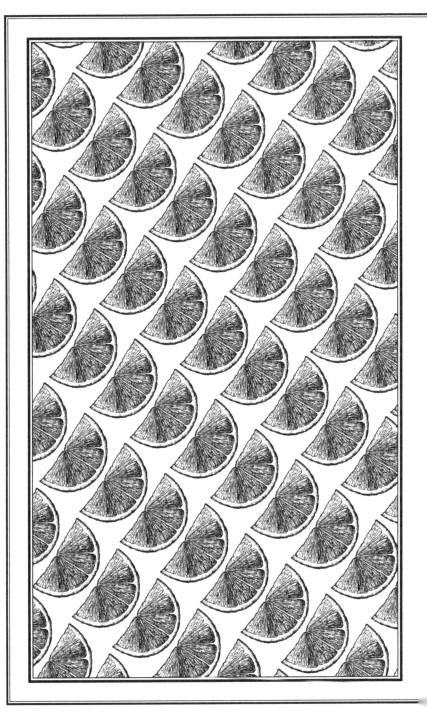

I

ICEBERG

IMPROVED WHISKEY
COCKTAIL

INFANTE

INSPIRATION

ITALIAN HEATHER

IVY GIMLET

ICEBERG

A Vodka Rocks, enlivened with the slightest waft of absinthe. The brightness of the lime garnish will really bring the drink to life.

2 MEASURES VODKA

1 TSP ABSINTHE (OR PERNOD)

LIME TWIST, TO GARNISH

Pour the vodka into an old-fashioned glass filled with cubed ice.
Add the absinthe, stir briefly and garnish with a lime twist.

IMPROVED WHISKEY COCKTAIL

A subtle, nuanced augmentation of chilled whiskey. A cocktail before cocktails existed. Heaven.

2 MEASURES RYE OR BOURBON
WHISKEY

½ MEASURE MARASCHINO

1 TSP ABSINTHE (OR PERNOD)

2 DASHES ANGOSTURA BITTERS

LEMON TWIST, TO GARNISH

Add all the ingredients to
an old-fashioned glass filled
with cubed ice, stir briefly
and garnish with a lemon
twist.

INFANTE

*An inspired riff on the Army
and Navy cocktail from the late
1990s, created by renowned New
York graffiti artist Giuseppe
Gonzalez while tending bar at
Dutch Kills.*

2 MEASURES GOLD TEQUILA

¾ MEASURE LIME JUICE

½ MEASURE ORGEAT

Add all the ingredients to
a cocktail shaker, shake and
strain into a rocks glass filled
with cubed ice.
No garnish.

INSPIRATION

*A wonderfully herbal dry
Martini. A simple twist of lime
brings an essential brightness.*

2 MEASURES VODKA

½ MEASURE DRY VERMOUTH

½ MEASURE BÉNÉDICTINE

LIME TWIST, TO GARNISH

Add all the ingredients to
a cocktail shaker or mixing
glass, and fill with cubed ice.
Stir for 30 seconds, and strain
into a chilled Martini glass.
Garnish with a lime twist.

ITALIAN HEATHER

*Neither a Rob Roy nor a Bobby
Burns, a dry Scotch Manhattan
combined with pleasant herbal
undertones.*

2 MEASURES SCOTTISH WHISKY

1 MEASURE GALLIANO

LEMON TWIST, TO GARNISH

Add all the ingredients to
a cocktail shaker or mixing
glass, and fill with cubed ice.
Stir for 30 seconds, and strain
into a chilled Martini glass.
Garnish with a lemon twist.

IVY GIMLET

*Like the Southside in style, or
a Cairpriaoska served "up" –
a handful of mint brings a
welcome freshness this bright
Vodka Sour.*

2 MEASURES VODKA

1 MEASURE LIME JUICE

¾ MEASURE SUGAR SYRUP

8 MINT LEAVES

LIME TWIST, TO GARNISH

Add all the ingredients to
your cocktail shaker, shake
vigorously and double strain
into a chilled coupette glass.
Garnish with a lime twist.

> *"The proper union of gin and vermouth is a great and sudden glory; it is one of the happiest marriages on earth, and one of the shortest lived."*

Bernard DeVoto

J

JACK ROSE

A snappy Applejack Sour from the 1930s, softened with the sweetness of grenadine and an attractive "rose" hue.

2 MEASURES APPLE BRANDY,
APPLEJACK OR CALVADOS
¾ MEASURE LEMON JUICE
½ MEASURE GRENADINE

Add all the ingredients to your cocktail shaker, shake vigorously and double strain into a chilled Martini glass. No garnish.

JAFFA

A creamy chocolate-orange dessert cocktail. Would also be great blended with a splash of whole milk and a handful of ice.

1 MEASURE COGNAC
1 MEASURE DARK CRÈME DE

CACAO

1 MEASURE DOUBLE CREAM

COCOA POWDER, TO GARNISH

Add all the ingredients to your cocktail shaker, shake vigorously and strain into a wine glass.
Garnish with a dusting of cocoa powder.

JALISCO

Jalisco is the birthplace and home of tequila and the third largest state in Mexico where the blue agave plant – from which tequila is derived – grows. Tequila is separated into three categories. Blanco (which is unaged), Reposado (aged in oak barrels from two months to one year) and Anejo (aged in oak barrels between one and three years). The town of Santiago de Tequila is a UNESCO World Heritage Site.

JALISCO SWIZZLE

A Mexican riff on the Mojito. Best enjoyed on a summer day, sombrero optional.

1 MEASURE TEQUILA

1 MEASURE GOLD RUM

1 MEASURE PASSION FRUIT JUICE

½ MEASURE LIME JUICE

¼ MEASURE SUGAR SYRUP

3 DASHES ANGOSTURA BITTERS

SODA WATER, TO TOP

TO GARNISH

LIME WEDGE

MINT SPRIG

Add all the ingredients except the soda water to a highball glass.
Fill the glass with crushed ice, and churn with a bar spoon.
Add a splash of soda water, and top up with more crushed ice.
Garnish with a lime wedge and a mint sprig.

JAPANESE COCKTAIL

First appearing in Jerry Thomas's "How to Mix Drinks" (1862), and said to be created to commemorate the occasion of an American diplomatic mission to Japan.

2½ MEASURES COGNAC
½ MEASURE ORGEAT
LEMON TWIST, TO GARNISH

Add all the ingredients to a cocktail shaker or mixing glass, and fill with cubed ice. Stir for 30 seconds, and strain into a coupette Martini glass. Garnish with a lemon twist.

JASMINE

Wonderfully dry and refreshing, with Campari adding a bitter complexity.

1½ MEASURES GIN
¾ MEASURE LEMON JUICE
¾ MEASURE COINTREAU
2 TSP CAMPARI
LEMON TWIST, TO GARNISH

Add all the ingredients to your cocktail shaker, shake vigorously and double strain into a chilled Martini glass. Garnish with a lemon twist.

JIGGER

A jigger is a type of metal cup used for measuring cocktail ingredients. They come in various shapes and sizes, and will include numbers denoting measurements of liquid volume. Jiggers are essential for accurate and consistent measuring of ingredients, which will always make your drink taste better. According to cocktail historian David Wondrich, the name simply derives from the American term "thingamajig".

JOURNALIST

A complex Martini from Harry Craddock. The additional bitters make this the perfect digestive cocktail for gin lovers.

2 MEASURES GIN
½ MEASURE DRY VERMOUTH
½ MEASURE SWEET VERMOUTH
1 TSP LEMON JUICE
2 DASHES ANGOSTURA BITTERS
2 DASHES ORANGE BITTERS
LEMON TWIST, TO GARNISH

Add all the ingredients to a cocktail shaker or mixing glass, and fill with cubed ice. Stir for 30 seconds, and strain into a Martini glass.
Garnish with a lemon twist.

JUNE BUG

Banana, melon and coconut combine to create sweet tropical silliness. Make sure you shake this really well, and go easy on the sugar.

1 MEASURE MIDORI
¾ MEASURE COCONUT RUM
¾ MEASURE BANANA LIQUEUR
¾ MEASURE LIME JUICE
½ MEASURE SUGAR SYRUP
3 MEASURES PINEAPPLE JUICE
PINEAPPLE LEAF, TO GARNISH

Add all the ingredients to your cocktail shaker, shake vigorously and strain into a hurricane glass filled with cubed ice.
Garnish with a pineapple leaf.

JUNGLE BIRD

A sublime and sophisticated bitter rum punch, created by Giuseppe Gonzalez in New York City. As always, but particularly with the Jungle Bird, using the very best and freshest ingredients you can will give you best results.

1½ MEASURES DARK RUM

½ MEASURE CAMPARI

1½ MEASURES PINEAPPLE JUICE

½ MEASURE LIME JUICE

½ MEASURE SUGAR SYRUP

LIME WEDGE, TO GARNISH

Add all the ingredients to
your cocktail shaker, shake
vigorously and double strain
into a rocks glass filled with
cubed ice.
Garnish with a lime wedge.

"I'm an occasional drinker, the kind of guy who goes out for a beer and wakes up in Singapore with a full beard."

Raymond Chandler, *Philip Marlowe's Guide to Life*

K

KENTUCKY RIVER

KING'S FIZZ

KIR ROYAL

KISS IN THE DARK

KIWI SMASH

KURANT BLUSH

KENTUCKY RIVER

Almost a chocolate Old Fashioned, but not quite. The peach brings a sweet, floral fragrance.

2 MEASURES BOURBON

½ MEASURE WHITE CRÈME DE CACAO

2 DASHES PEACH BITTERS

LEMON TWIST, TO GARNISH

Add all the ingredients to an old-fashioned glass filled with cubed ice.
Stir well, and garnish with a lemon twist.

KING'S FIZZ

A Gin Fizz spiked with orange bitters which lift all ingredients and give a fantastic citric intensity. The "dry shake" is essential for achieving the desired light and fluffy texture.

2 MEASURES GIN

1 MEASURE LEMON JUICE

¾ MEASURE SUGAR SYRUP

½ MEASURE EGG WHITE

2 DASHES ORANGE BITTERS

SODA WATER, TO TOP

Add all the ingredients except the soda water to your cocktail shaker and vigorously "dry shake" without ice for 10 seconds. Take the shaker apart, add cubed ice and shake vigorously.
Strain into a chilled highball glass and top with soda water.
No ice, no garnish.

KIR ROYAL

A classic celebratory aperitif, French in origin and loved the world over.

1 MEASURE CRÈME DE CASSIS

CHILLED SPARKLING WINE, TO

TOP

Pour the crème de cassis into a Champagne flute and top with sparkling wine.

KISS IN THE DARK

A satisfyingly strong and fruited Gin Martini with floral wine notes. To fully enjoy this must be stirred properly, so the cherry brandy can open up and dilute sufficiently. Tasty.

1½ MEASURES GIN

1 MEASURE CHERRY BRANDY

1 MEASURE DRY VERMOUTH

LEMON TWIST, TO GARNISH

Add all the ingredients to a cocktail shaker or mixing glass, and fill with cubed ice. Stir for 30 seconds, and strain into a chilled coupette glass. Garnish with a lemon twist.

KIWI SMASH

A citric, emerald green Vodka Fix. An exotic summery alternative to the Caiprioska.

2 MEASURES VODKA
¾ MEASURE LIME JUICE
½ MEASURE SUGAR SYRUP
1 KIWI FRUIT, PEELED AND
CUBED
LIME WEDGE, TO GARNISH

Drop the kiwi fruit into a rocks glass, and muddle with a spoon.
Add the remaining ingredients, fill the glass with crushed ice and churn.
Top with more crushed ice and garnish with a lime wedge.

1½ MEASURES BLACKCURRANT
VODKA
½ MEASURE STRAWBERRY
LIQUEUR
1½ MEASURES CRANBERRY
JUICE
½ MEASURE LIME JUICE
TO GARNISH
REDCURRANT STRING
ORANGE TWIST

Add all the ingredients to your cocktail shaker, shake vigorously and double strain into a chilled Martini glass. Garnish with a string of redcurrants and an orange twist.

KURANT BLUSH

A sweet and fruity alternative to the Cosmopolitan, while retaining an appealing sharpness.

"Never trust any complicated cocktail that remains perfectly clear until the last ingredient goes in, and then immediately clouds."

Terry Pratchett

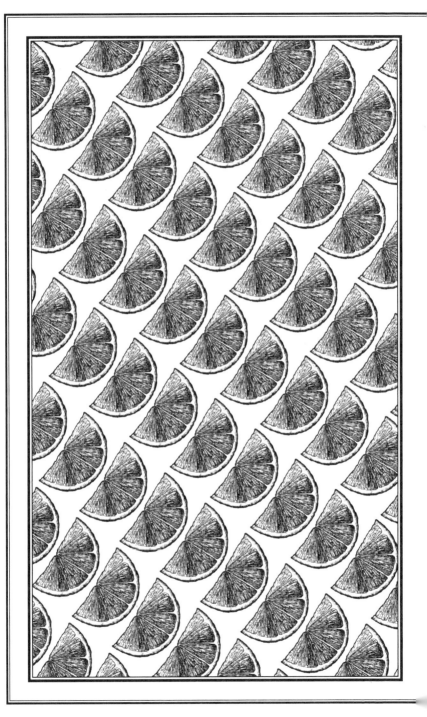

L

LE MANS

LEMONGRASS COLLINS

LIMON MOJITO

LITTLE ITALY

LOLA'S PUNCH

LONDON CALLING

LONG ISLAND ICED TEA

LOS ALTOS

LOVING CUP

LYCHEE MARTINI

LE MANS

A simple but effective improvement on the Vodka Soda. Its low alcohol content makes it a fantastic summer afternoon session drink.

1 MEASURE VODKA

1 MEASURE COINTREAU

SODA WATER, TO TOP

LEMON WEDGE, TO GARNISH

Add the vodka and Cointreau to a rocks glass filled with cubed ice. Top with soda water and garnish with a lemon wedge.

LEMONGRASS COLLINS

A sweetly spiced and aromatic Collins with an Asian twist. The lemongrass brings a fresh and delicate zing.

2 MEASURES VODKA

¾ MEASURE LEMON JUICE

½ MEASURE VANILLA SYRUP

½ STICK LEMONGRASS, CHOPPED

GINGER BEER, TO TOP

LEMON WEDGE, TO GARNISH

Add all the ingredients except the ginger beer to your cocktail shaker. Shake and double strain into a highball glass filled with cubed ice, top with ginger beer and garnish with a lemon wedge.

8 LEAVES MINT

SODA WATER, TO TOP

TO GARNISH

LIME WEDGES

LEMON WEDGES

MINT SPRIG

Add all the ingredients except the soda water to a highball glass and fill the glass with crushed ice, and churn with a bar spoon. Add a splash of soda water, and top up with more crushed ice. Garnish with lime and lemon wedges and a mint sprig.

LIMON MOJITO

A twist on the Mojito, given a sharp southern Italian kick by the limoncello. The caster sugar provides a satisfying sweet crunch.

1 MEASURE WHITE RUM

1 MEASURE LIMONCELLO

½ MEASURE LIME JUICE

½ MEASURE LEMON JUICE

1 TSP CASTER SUGAR

LITTLE ITALY

A stunning Manhattan alternative, with rich and bitter notes of artichoke from the Cynar. Created by Audrey Saunders at the Pegu Club in New York City.

2 MEASURES RYE WHISKEY

½ MEASURE SWEET VERMOUTH

½ MEASURE CYNAR

ORANGE TWIST, TO GARNISH

Add all the ingredients to a cocktail shaker or mixing glass, and fill with cubed ice. Stir for 30 seconds, and strain into a chilled coupette glass. Garnish with an orange twist.

LOLA'S PUNCH

MAKES 1 JUG

Intense mango and apple, and the sharp fruitiness of white wine, make for a crisp and perfectly balanced summer sharer.

4 MEASURES WHITE RUM

3 MEASURES LEMON JUICE

3 MEASURES SUGAR SYRUP

3 MEASURES APPLE JUICE

3 MEASURES MANGO JUICE

⅓ BOTTLE WHITE WINE

SODA WATER, TO TOP

TO GARNISH

APPLE SLICES

MANGO SLICES

Add all the ingredients to a jug or punch bowl filled with cubed ice and stir well.

Garnish with slices of apple and mango and serve in wine glasses.

LONDON CALLING

Created by Christopher Jepson in 2002 at London's Milk and Honey, and now something of a contemporary classic. The sea-salt salinity of sherry provides a complex, dry background to the classic Gin Sour. Fantastic.

1½ MEASURES GIN

¾ MEASURE LEMON JUICE

¾ MEASURE FINO SHERRY

½ MEASURE SUGAR SYRUP

2 DASHES ANGOSTURA BITTERS

LEMON TWIST, TO GARNISH

Add all the ingredients to your cocktail shaker, shake vigorously and strain into a chilled coupette glass. Garnish with a lemon twist.

LONG ISLAND ICED TEA

Rising to fame in the 1980s and still enormously popular today, the Long Island Iced Tea takes the most well-known light spirits and sweetens them with cola. A perfectly permissible guilty pleasure.

½ MEASURE VODKA

½ MEASURE GIN

½ MEASURE WHITE RUM

½ MEASURE TEQUILA

½ MEASURE TRIPLE SEC

¾ MEASURE LEMON JUICE

½ MEASURE SUGAR SYRUP

COLA, TO TOP

LEMON WEDGE, TO GARNISH

Add all the ingredients except the cola to your cocktail shaker, shake and strain into a hurricane glass filled with cubed ice and top with cola.
Garnish with a lemon wedge.

LOS ALTOS

A Tequila Collins with a bitter Campari kick. Sharp and clean flavours for the culturally confused. Lovely.

2 MEASURES TEQUILA

½ MEASURE LIME JUICE

2 MEASURES ORANGE JUICE

3 TSP AGAVE SYRUP

2 TSP CAMPARI

SODA WATER, TO TOP

TO GARNISH

LIME WEDGE

ORANGE SLICE

Add all the ingredients except the soda to your cocktail shaker, shake and strain into a hurricane glass filled with cubed ice and top with soda water.
Garnish with a lime wedge and a slice of orange.

LOVING CUP

MAKES 1 JUG

A sweet and boozy sharing punch. Can be prepared in moments and perfect at Christmas.

½ BOTTLE SWEET SHERRY

¼ BOTTLE COGNAC

1 BOTTLE PROSECCO

4 MEASURES LEMON JUICE

2 MEASURES SUGAR SYRUP

TO GARNISH

ORANGE SLICES

LEMON SLICES

MINT SPRIGS

Add all the ingredients to a jug or punch bowl filled with cubed ice and stir well. Garnish with slices of orange and lemon and sprigs of mint and serve in wine glasses.

LYCHEE MARTINI

A product of the fruited Martini craze of the late 1990s in New York City, and a precursor to the craft cocktail revolution as a whole. Shake this really one well, to cut the cloying sweetness of lychee. A modern classic.

1½ MEASURES VODKA

1 MEASURE LYCHEE LIQUEUR

½ MEASURE LYCHEE SYRUP

(FROM A TIN OF LYCHEES)

¾ MEASURE LEMON JUICE

TINNED LYCHEES, TO GARNISH

Add all the ingredients to your cocktail shaker, shake vigorously and double strain into a chilled Martini glass. Garnish with the lychees.

TEQUILA: *"the steering liquor."*

Ernest Hemingway

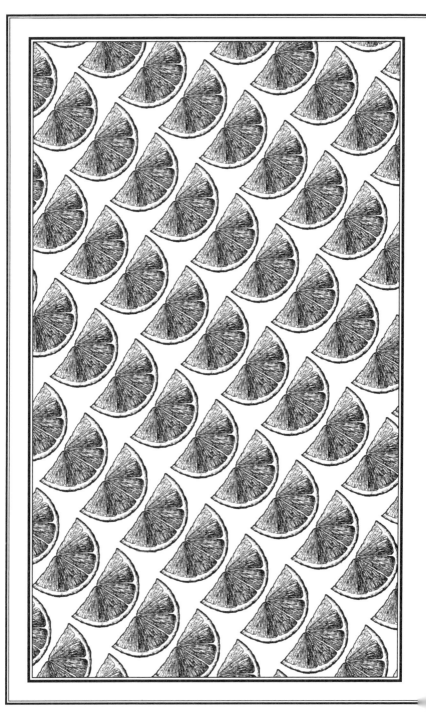

MACHETE

MAID

MANHATTAN

MANHATTAN

MARASCHINO

MARGARITA

MARTINEZ

MARTINI

MARTINI

MICHELADA

MINT JULEP

MOJITO

MONKEY GLAND

MOONSHINE

MOSCOW MULE

MUDSLIDE

MACHETE

Pineapple and tonic make for an intriguing and delicious combination. A sophisticated spirit and mixer-type sipper, and highly recommended.

2 MEASURES VODKA

3 MEASURES PINEAPPLE JUICE

TONIC WATER, TO TOP

LIME WEDGE, TO GARNISH

Add the vodka and pineapple juice to a highball glass filled with cubed ice.
Stir briefly, top up with the tonic water and garnish with a lime wedge.

MAID

Maids are a group of Sour-type cocktails, shaken vigorously with fresh cucumber and mint. Light and refreshing, with crisp and clean flavours, this is the classic gin version.

2 MEASURES GIN

1 MEASURE LIME JUICE

¾ MEASURE SUGAR SYRUP

3 CUBES CUCUMBER

8 MINT LEAVES

TO GARNISH

CUCUMBER SLICES

MINT SPRIG

Add all the ingredients to your cocktail shaker, shake vigorously and double strain into an old-fashioned glass filled with cubed ice. Garnish with sliced cucumber and a mint sprig.

MANHATTAN

Steeped in history, and a building block of classic cocktail making. It is often incorrectly stated that the Manhattan was created for Lady Randolph Churchill (mother of Winston) in 1874. Debate as to its true origin is ongoing but, as with the Martinez cocktail, one might assume that the Manhattan would predate the Martini, due to the simple fact that that Italian (or sweet) vermouth arrived in the United States some years before French (or dry) vermouth did.

MANHATTAN

The rich wine notes from sweet vermouth, combined which the spice and punch of rye whiskey are what give the drink such depth and complexity. A touch of dry vermouth could also be added, making it a perfect Manhattan. Stirred down and meaningful.

2 MEASURES RYE WHISKEY

1 MEASURE SWEET VERMOUTH

2 DASHES ANGOSTURA BITTERS

TO GARNISH

COCKTAIL CHERRY

ORANGE TWIST

Add all the ingredients to a cocktail shaker or mixing glass, and fill with cubed ice. Stir for 30 seconds, and strain into a chilled coupette glass. Garnish with a cocktail cherry and an orange twist.

MARASCHINO

Maraschino is a liqueur made with Marasca cherries, from which its name derives. Intensely flavoured, it is an extremely useful ingredient when used sparingly, giving a bittersweet depth and complexity to classic cocktails. The most widely used brand would be Luxardo Maraschino, originating in 1821 on the Italian Dalmatian coast.

MARGARITA

Simply a Tequila Sour with an orange kick, the Margarita is a global favourite, with countless styles and variations. The version below is sharp, sour and potent.

1½ MEASURES GOLD TEQUILA

1 MEASURE COINTREAU

1 MEASURE LIME JUICE, PLUS EXTRA TO FROST (OPTIONAL)

1 TBSP SUGAR SYRUP

SALT, TO FROST (OPTIONAL)

LIME WEDGE, TO GARNISH

If you wish, dip the rim of a Margarita glass in lime juice, then into salt to create a salt frosting.
Add all the ingredients to your cocktail shaker, shake vigorously and double strain into the prepared glass. Garnish with a lime wedge on the side of the glass.

MARTINEZ

Conceived in around 1870, supposedly in northern California, a sweeter and more complex precursor to the Martini Cocktail. Stunning.

2 MEASURES GIN

1 MEASURE SWEET VERMOUTH

1 TSP MARASCHINO

2 DASHES ANGOSTURA BITTERS

ORANGE TWIST, TO GARNISH

Add all the ingredients to a cocktail shaker or mixing glass, and fill with cubed ice.

Stir for 30 seconds, and strain into a chilled coupette glass. Garnish with an orange twist.

MARTINI

The quintessence of elegant drinking, drinking a classic Martini is a deeply personal experience. Regardless of your spirit, vermouth and garnish preference, which will and should differ from person to person, below is a recipe for a crisp and balanced classic Gin Martini.

2½ MEASURES GIN

½ MEASURE DRY VERMOUTH

1 DASH ORANGE BITTERS

LEMON TWIST OR OLIVE, TO GARNISH

Add all the ingredients to a cocktail shaker or mixing glass, and fill with cubed ice. Stir for 30 seconds, and strain into a chilled Martini glass. Garnish with your preference of a lemon twist or olive.

MARTINI

Originating in the United States in the mid- to late 1800s, the Dry Martini gained mass exposure in the 1920s, by which time the recipe had embedded itself into the public consciousness. Prohibition furthered its popularity, with the vermouth used to mask the unpleasant impurities of poorly made illegal "bathtub" gin – spawning the concept of a "wet" Martini, meaning simply that more vermouth was stirred into the drink than before. A dash of orange bitters, and a simple garnish of an olive or lemon twist completes the classic recipe.

MICHELADA

A rough and tumble beery Mexican Bloody Mary of sorts. The hot sauce element can be of your personal choosing, but the general idea is that this is a drink that should be assembled quickly and imbibed in minimum time, ideally under the beating sun.

1 MEASURE LIME JUICE, PLUS EXTRA FOR FROSTING

1 MEASURE HOT SAUCE

1 MEASURE TOMATO JUICE

COLD LAGER, TO TOP

SALT, FOR FROSTING

Dip the rim of a highball glass in lime juice, then into the salt to create a salt rim. Add all of the ingredients to the prepared glass.

MINT JULEP

This southern United States classic was the official drink of the Kentucky Derby in the 1930s, but Juleps have been sipped for medicinal purposes for centuries. A sort of Whiskey Mojito, this is a celebration drink to get dressed up for on a summer afternoon.

2 MEASURES BOURBON

2 TSP SUGAR SYRUP

8 MINT LEAVES

3 DASHES ANGOSTURA BITTERS

MINT SPRIGS, TO GARNISH

Add all the ingredients to a rocks glass (or Julep cup) filled with crushed ice. Churn vigorously, top with more crushed ice and garnish with 2–3 mint sprigs.

MOJITO

The combination of lime, sugar and "aguardiente" (a crude form of rum) can be traced back to the 15th century in Cuba, used as a tonic against scurvy. Over time, the quality of rum improved, and the Mojito became the global favourite it is today.

2 MEASURES WHITE RUM

8 MINT LEAVES

8 LIME WEDGES

2 TSP CASTER SUGAR

SODA WATER, TO TOP

MINT SPRIG, TO GARNISH

Muddle the mint, lime and sugar in the bottom of a highball glass with a rolling pin, add the rum and stir well.

Fill the glass with crushed ice, and churn vigorously.

Top with more crushed ice and a splash of soda water and garnish with a mint sprig.

MONKEY GLAND

An amusingly named gin cocktail, originating at Harry's New York Bar, Paris, in the 1920s.

2 MEASURES GIN

1 MEASURE ORANGE JUICE

1 TBSP GRENADINE

2 DROPS ABSINTHE OR PERNOD

Add all the ingredients to your cocktail shaker, shake vigorously and strain into a chilled coupette glass.
No garnish.

MOONSHINE

Moonshine was the name given to illegally produced high alcohol spirits produced in North America from the mid-1800s onwards, most likely brought over by Irish immigrants and usually produced illicitly in people's homes. Essentially an unaged and therefore colourless whiskey, its production and consumption were fraught with danger and health risks.

MOSCOW MULE

Originating in North America, though argument still rages as to where, the Moscow Mule is highly drinkable extension of a Vodka Highball.

2 MEASURES VODKA

1 MEASURE LIME JUICE

GINGER BEER, TO TOP

TO GARNISH

LIME WEDGE

MINT SPRIG

Add the vodka and lime juice to a highball glass filled with cubed ice, top with ginger beer and garnish with a lime wedge and a sprig of mint.

MUDSLIDE

A decadent (though calorific) after-dinner treat of coffee and cream and far tastier than its name suggests.

1 MEASURE VODKA

1 MEASURE KAHLÚA

1 MEASURE BAILEYS IRISH

CREAM

COCOA POWDER, TO GARNISH

Add all the ingredients to your cocktail shaker, shake vigorously and strain into a chilled wine glass. Garnish with a dusting of cocoa powder.

"A perfect Martini should be made by filling a glass with gin then waving it in the general direction of Italy."

Noël Coward

N

NEGRONI

NEVADA COCKTAIL

NEW ORLEANS DRY MARTINI

NEW YORK SOUR

NEGRONI

Created in Florence in 1919 when the Count Camillo Negroni requested a slug of gin be added to his Americano cocktail. Though arguably an acquired taste initially, the intense bitter complexity of the Negroni is an unrivalled pleasure.

1 MEASURE GIN

1 MEASURE CAMPARI

1 MEASURE SWEET VERMOUTH

ORANGE SLICE, TO GARNISH

Pour all the ingredients into a rocks glass filled with ice. Stir briefly, and garnish with an orange slice.

NEVADA COCKTAIL

An "improved" Daiquiri, with grapefruit providing length and bitterness. First published in "The Savoy Cocktail Book" (1930).

2 MEASURES WHITE RUM

1 MEASURE PINK GRAPEFRUIT JUICE

¾ MEASURE LIME JUICE

¾ MEASURE SUGAR SYRUP

2 DASHES ANGOSTURA BITTERS

LIME WEDGE, TO GARNISH

Add all the ingredients to your cocktail shaker, shake vigorously and double strain into a chilled coupette glass. Garnish with a lime wedge on the side of the glass.

NEW ORLEANS DRY MARTINI

A bone-dry Gin Martini, with a snap of anise coming from the absinthe – a nod to the city's French heritage. A drink to whet the appetite before dinner, in New Orleans ideally.

2½ MEASURES GIN

½ MEASURE DRY VERMOUTH

2 DROPS ABSINTHE OR PERNOD

LEMON TWIST, TO GARNISH

Add all the ingredients to a cocktail shaker or mixing glass filled with cubed ice. Stir for 30 seconds and strain into a chilled Martini glass. Garnish with a twist of lemon.

NEW YORK SOUR

A classic Whiskey Sour with red wine floated prettily over the top, for a luxurious tannic finish. Excellent.

2 MEASURES BOURBON

¾ MEASURE LEMON JUICE

¾ MEASURE SUGAR SYRUP

½ MEASURE EGG WHITE

1 MEASURE RED WINE

LEMON WEDGE, TO GARNISH

Add all the ingredients except the red wine to your cocktail shaker and "dry shake" without ice for 10 seconds, then take the shaker apart and add cubed ice. Shake vigorously and double strain into an old-fashioned glass filled with cubed ice, then carefully pour over the red wine.
Garnish with a lemon wedge.

O

OLD CUBAN

OLD FASHIONED

OLD FASHIONED

OLD PAL

ON THE LAWN

OPERA

ORANGE BLOSSOM

ORCHARD COLLINS

ORGEAT

ORIGINAL PISCO SOUR

OYSTER SHOT

OLD CUBAN

A delightful halfway house between a Daiquiri and a Mojito, freshened with a splash of Champagne; created by Audrey Saunders at the Pegu Club in New York City. Utterly delicious.

1½ MEASURES WHITE RUM

¾ MEASURE LIME JUICE

¾ MEASURE SUGAR SYRUP

2 DASHES ANGOSTURA BITTERS

6 MINTS LEAVES, PLUS AN

EXTRA LEAF TO GARNISH

CHILLED CHAMPAGNE, TO TOP

Add all the ingredients except the Champagne to your cocktail shaker, shake vigorously and double strain into a chilled coupette glass. Top with a splash of Champagne and garnish with a mint leaf.

OLD FASHIONED

A cocktail made "the old-fashioned way" entailed simply a base spirit, sugar, water and bitters; so the Old Fashioned might be considered a style of drink as much as a stand-alone serve. Brought to global fame as Don Draper's drink of choice in the 1960s'-set television show "Mad Men", its origins are in fact rooted in the 1880s at the Pendennis Club in Louisville, Kentucky.

OLD FASHIONED

Rich, complex and strong. The Old Fashioned cocktail rightly sits among the truly great drink creations of all time. Its genius lies in its simplicity, though be careful to make the drink with the utmost care and patience. Worth the wait.

2 MEASURES BOURBON

1 TBSP SUGAR SYRUP

3 DASHES ANGOSTURA BITTERS

ORANGE TWIST, TO GARNISH

Add all the ingredients to an old-fashioned glass and add 5–6 cubes of ice.
Stir continuously for 30 seconds, gradually adding in more ice, 1 cube at a time.
Garnish with an orange twist.

OLD PAL

A bracing dry Manhattan, with a strong bitter element provided by Campari. Said to have originated in Paris in the 1920s at Harry's New York Bar.

1½ MEASURES RYE WHISKEY

¾ MEASURE DRY VERMOUTH

½ MEASURE CAMPARI

LEMON TWIST, TO GARNISH

Add all the ingredients to a cocktail shaker or mixing glass filled with cubed ice. Stir for 30 seconds and strain into a chilled Martini glass. Garnish with a twist of lemon.

ON THE LAWN

An extension of Pimm's and lemonade by way of gin and ginger ale, perfect to share on a summer afternoon.

1 MEASURE PIMM'S NO. 1 CUP

1 MEASURE GIN

2 MEASURES LEMONADE

2 MEASURES GINGER ALE

TO GARNISH

CUCUMBER SLICES

ORANGE SLICES

STRAWBERRIES

Add all the ingredients to a highball glass filled with cubed ice, and stir. Garnish with slices of cucumber, orange and strawberries.

OPERA

An elegant, softer interpretation of the Martinez cocktail. The commonly made version appears in "The Savoy Cocktail Book" (1930), which uses maraschino

instead of an orange liqueur. The recipe below is nearer to the original one, appearing in Jacques Straub's "Straub's Manual of Mixed Drinks" (1913).

1½ MEASURES GIN

1 MEASURE DUBONNET

½ MEASURE ORANGE LIQUEUR

1 DASH ANGOSTURA BITTERS

ORANGE TWIST, TO GARNISH

Add all the ingredients to a cocktail shaker or mixing glass filled with cubed ice. Stir for 30 seconds and strain into a chilled Martini glass. Garnish with an orange twist.

ORANGE BLOSSOM

A sharply citric gin snifter, with orgeat providing a nutty almond warmth and depth.

2 MEASURES GIN

2 MEASURES PINK GRAPEFRUIT
JUICE

2 TSP ORGEAT

2 DASHES ANGOSTURA BITTERS

4 ORANGE SLICES, PLUS EXTRA
TO GARNISH

Muddle the orange slices
and orgeat in a rocks glass
with the bottom of a rolling
pin, add the remaining
ingredients, fill with crushed
ice and churn.
Top with more crushed ice
and garnish with a slice of
orange.

½ MEASURE ELDERFLOWER
CORDIAL

2 MEASURES APPLE JUICE

CIDER, TO TOP

TO GARNISH

APPLE SLICES

LEMON SLICES

Add all the ingredients
except the cider to your
cocktail shaker, shake and
strain into a highball glass
filled with cubed ice.
Top with cider and garnish
with slices of apple and
lemon.

ORCHARD COLLINS

A bright and autumnal Collins-style cooler, with warm flavours of the British orchard. Cider brings a pleasant and unexpected dryness. Lovely.

2 MEASURES GIN

¾ MEASURE LEMON JUICE

ORGEAT

Orgeat is a syrup or cordial made by combining almonds, sugar and water. Rose water or orange flower may also be added to create a sweet and fragrant syrup that tastes not dissimilar to marzipan. When used sparingly, it makes for an excellent and versatile cocktail modifier.

ORIGINAL PISCO SOUR

Pisco is a type of South American brandy most typically ascribed to Peru. Rougher than Cognac, and closer to rum in taste, it makes for a stunning Sour. A contemporary classic.

2 MEASURES PISCO

1 MEASURE LEMON JUICE

¾ MEASURE SUGAR SYRUP

½ MEASURE EGG WHITE

2 DASHES ANGOSTURA BITTERS

LEMON WEDGE, TO GARNISH

Add all the ingredients to your cocktail shaker and "dry shake" without ice for 10 seconds, then take the shaker apart and add cubed ice. Shake vigorously and strain into an old-fashioned glass filled with cubed ice. Garnish with a lemon wedge.

OYSTER SHOT

A somewhat extreme hangover cure. A quick shot of Bloody Mary, intensified with a freshly shucked oyster. Great fun, but not for the fainthearted.

¾ MEASURE VODKA

¾ MEASURE TOMATO JUICE

4 DROPS TABASCO SAUCE

3 DASHES WORCESTERSHIRE SAUCE

PINCH OF CELERY SALT

PINCH OF BLACK PEPPER

1 FRESH OYSTER

Add all the ingredients except the oyster to your cocktail shaker, shake vigorously and double strain into a rocks glass. Drop in the oyster, close your eyes and knock it back.

"Got tight last night on absinthe and did knife tricks. Great success shooting the knife underhand into the piano."

Ernest Hemingway in a letter to a friend in 1931

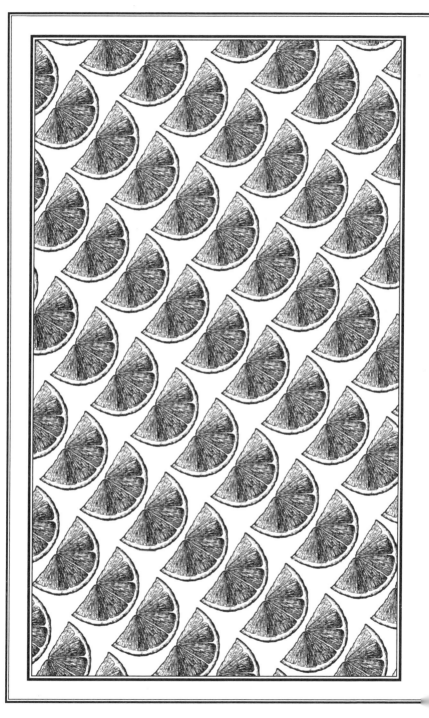

P

Q

P

PALOMA

Straight from the beaches of Mexico – this is a perfect summer Highball, simple to create and dangerously drinkable.

2 MEASURES TEQUILA

¾ MEASURE LIME JUICE

GRAPEFRUIT SODA, TO TOP

LIME WEDGE, TO GARNISH

Add all the ingredients to a highball glass filled with cubed ice, top with grapefruit soda and garnish with a lime wedge.

PASSION FRUIT MARGARITA

Sharp citrus and tropical flavours combine in this summer alternative to the classic Margarita.

1½ MEASURES GOLD TEQUILA

1 MEASURE COINTREAU

¾ MEASURE LIME JUICE, PLUS
EXTRA TO FROST (OPTIONAL)

½ MEASURE PASSION FRUIT
SYRUP

PULP AND SEEDS OF 1 PASSION
FRUIT

SALT, TO FROST (OPTIONAL)

LIME WEDGE, TO GARNISH

If you wish, dip the rim of a
Margarita glass in lime juice,
then into salt to create a salt
frosting.
Add all the ingredients to
your cocktail shaker, shake
vigorously and strain into the
prepared glass.
Garnish with a lime wedge
on the side of the glass.

PERFECT LADY

*An elegant and floral Gin Sour
perfumed with peach. Created at
the Grosvenor House Hotel,
London, in 1936 by Sidney Cox.
A sublime and underappreciated
classic.*

1½ MEASURES GIN

¾ MEASURE LEMON JUICE

½ MEASURE PEACH LIQUEUR

½ MEASURE EGG WHITE

Add all the ingredients to
your cocktail shaker and
vigorously "dry shake"
without ice for 10 seconds.
Take the shaker apart,
add cubed ice and shake
vigorously.
Double strain into a chilled
coupette glass.
No garnish.

PIMM'S CUP

*A sensational British aperitif,
rightly still enjoyed every
summer. Feel free to be creative
with your fruit garnishing –
anything goes.*

2 MEASURES PIMM'S NO. 1 CUP

GINGER ALE, TO TOP

TO GARNISH

CUCUMBER SLICE

SLICED STRAWBERRIES

MINT SPRIG

Add all the ingredients to a highball glass filled with cubed ice and garnish a slice of cucumber, sliced strawberries and a mint sprig.

PIÑA COLADA

Smooth, sweet and creamy. The pride of Puerto Rico, sung and written about since its conception in the 1950s, and a treat that never disappoints. Take me to the beach and give me a Piña Colada. Please.

2 MEASURES LIGHT RUM

2 MEASURES COCONUT CREAM

6 CHUNKS FRESH PINEAPPLE

PINEAPPLE LEAF, TO GARNISH

Add all ingredients with 7 cubes of ice to a blender or food processor and blend until smooth.
Pour into a hurricane glass and garnish with a pineapple leaf.

PINK GIN

Sounding more appealing than it possibly is, and vastly popular in its day. The Pink Gin was conceived by naval officers in Plymouth in the mid-1800s as a means of making a tonic prescribed for sea sickness more palatable – that tonic was none other than Angostura bitters.

2 MEASURES GIN

5 DASHES ANGOSTURA BITTERS

STILL WATER, TO TOP

Add all ingredients to an old-fashioned glass filled with cubed ice and stir briefly. No garnish.

PINK SANGRIA

Floral and pleasantly fruited, lemon verbena tea brings depth and tannic complexity. A low-alcohol summer cooler.

2 MEASURES ROSÉ WINE

1½ MEASURES POMEGRANATE JUICE

1½ MEASURES COLD LEMON VERBENA TEA

2 TSP AGAVE SYRUP

SODA WATER, TO TOP

PINK GRAPEFRUIT SLICE, TO GARNISH

Add all ingredients to a wine glass filled with cubed ice. Stir briefly and garnish with a slice of pink grapefruit.

2 MEASURES STILL WATER

3 DASHES ANGOSTURA BITTERS

TO GARNISH

ORANGE SLICE

MINT SPRIG

Add all the ingredients to your cocktail shaker, shake and strain into a highball glass filled with cubed ice and garnish with a slice of orange and a sprig of mint.

Planter's Punch

Though rum based, the Planter's Punch was in fact created in South Carolina. Now adapted and acknowledged as a fruit-led rum punch, the recipe here is nearer to the original.

2 MEASURES DARK JAMAICAN RUM

½ MEASURE LIME JUICE

1 MEASURE SUGAR SYRUP

PROHIBITION

In response to rising social difficulties stemming from the misuse of alcohol in the United States, The Volstead Act of 1920 prohibited the production, importation, transportation and sale of alcohol. In a sense it worked, as alcohol consumption dropped markedly. However, what it gave birth to was an underground crime wave, driven predominantly by the illegal smuggling and production of alcohol. Prohibition was ended in 1933 by President Roosevelt.

PROOF

Proof, or alcohol by volume (ABV), as it is known in Europe, measures the alcohol percentage present within alcoholic liquids. This enables governments to apply the appropriate tax to specific products, while informing the drinker as to the actual alcoholic strength of what they are consuming.

PUNCH

Derived from the Sanskrit word meaning "five", a traditional punch was a drink served to a group of people in some form of sharing vessel, usually a bowl or a jug. Its base components would always be alcohol, citrus juice, sugar, water, and then a fifth flavouring which was more often than not tea or fruit juice. Punches are part of most cultural vernaculars, and are usually made and served to mark special occasions.

QUEEN MOTHER COCKTAIL

Widely reported as Elizabeth Bowes-Lyon's favourite tipple, taken regularly to aid longevity. Miss Bowes-Lyon was more widely known by her formal title, The Queen Mother.

2 MEASURES DUBONNET

1 MEASURE GIN

LEMON SLICE, TO GARNISH

Add both ingredients to an old-fashioned glass filled with cubed ice, stir briefly and garnish with a slice of lemon.

R

RED CLOUD

RHETT BUTLER

RITZ OLD FASHIONED

ROB ROY

ROSSINI

RUDE COSMOPOLITAN

RUM

RUM OLD FASHIONED

RUM SOUR

RUSSIAN SPRING PUNCH

RUSTY NAIL

RYE

RED CLOUD

A Gin Sour, sweetened with apricot and grenadine and sharpened with bitters.

1½ MEASURES GIN

½ MEASURE APRICOT LIQUEUR

¾ MEASURE LEMON JUICE

I TSP GRENADINE

2 DASHES ANGOSTURA BITTERS

LEMON TWIST, TO GARNISH

Add all the ingredients to your cocktail shaker, shake and double strain into a chilled coupette glass. Garnish with a lemon twist.

RHETT BUTLER

More complex than it appears, with a sweetness coming from the bourbon and a pleasing astringency from the cranberry.

1½ MEASURES BOURBON

1 MEASURE ORANGE CURAÇAO

1 TSP LIME JUICE

1 TSP SUGAR SYRUP

4 MEASURES CRANBERRY JUICE

LIME WEDGE, TO GARNISH

Add all the ingredients to
your cocktail shaker, shake
and strain into a rocks glass
filled with ice.
Garnish with a lime wedge.

RITZ OLD FASHIONED

*A decadent version of the
Sidecar, with bourbon replacing
Cognac and Champagne notes
of Grand Marnier.*

1½ MEASURES BOURBON

½ MEASURE GRAND MARNIER

¾ MEASURE LEMON JUICE, PLUS
EXTRA FOR FROSTING

CASTER SUGAR, FOR FROSTING

EGG WHITE

LEMON TWIST, TO GARNISH

Frost the rim of a chilled
coupette glass in a touch of
lemon juice, then press it into
the caster sugar.
Add all the ingredients to
a cocktail shaker, shake and
strain into the prepared glass.
Garnish with a lemon twist.

ROB ROY

*Simply put; a Scotch
Manhattan, with a floral flavour
profile laced with heather honey.
Created in 1894 at the Waldorf
Astoria Hotel, New York, to
celebrate the premiere of the new
operetta Rob Roy.*

2 MEASURES SCOTCH WHISKY

1 MEASURE SWEET VERMOUTH

2 DASHES ANGOSTURA BITTERS

LEMON TWIST, TO GARNISH

Add all the ingredients to
a mixing glass or cocktail
shaker and fill with ice.
Gently stir with a bar spoon
for 20 seconds and strain into
a chilled Martini glass.
Garnish with a lemon twist.

ROSSINI

A sweeter strawberry alternative to the traditional peach-flavoured Bellini, and named after the Italian composer Gioachino Rossini.

4 STRAWBERRIES
1 TSP SUGAR SYRUP
CHILLED PROSECCO, TO TOP

Add the strawberries and sugar syrup to a blender or food processor and blend until smooth.
Pour into a Champagne flute and top with the chilled Prosecco.

RUDE COSMOPOLITAN

A Cosmopolitan made with a tequila. Or a Margarita with cranberry juice. Fun.

1½ MEASURES TEQUILA
1 MEASURE COINTREAU
1 MEASURE CRANBERRY JUICE
½ MEASURE LIME JUICE
LIME WEDGE DUSTED IN SEA SALT, TO GARNISH

Add all the ingredients to your cocktail shaker, shake vigorously and double strain into a chilled coupette glass. Garnish with a lime wedge dusted in sea salt.

RUM
Rum is a probably the broadest and most diverse of all the spirit categories. It is produced all over the world, though would most commonly be associated with Latin America and the Caribbean where the majority of it is produced. Rum is made by fermenting and distilling sugar cane by-products, most commonly either the molasses or the sugar cane juice itself, and then usually aged in oak barrels. Rum is the fascinating, ultimately unknowable

liquid traversing cultures and geography throughout history.

RUM OLD FASHIONED

Being darker and richer than American whiskey, the chocolate, coffee and ripe fruit notes from good-quality rum make for a superb Old Fashioned.

2 MEASURES AGED RUM

1 TSP SUGAR SYRUP

1 DASH ANGOSTURA BITTERS

1 DASH ORANGE BITTERS

LIME TWIST, TO GARNISH

Add all the ingredients to an old-fashioned glass and add 5–6 cubes of ice.
Stir continuously for 30 seconds, gradually adding in more ice, 1 cube at a time.
Garnish with a lime twist.

RUM SOUR

A complex and delicious Sour for rum lovers, and a great alternative to the Pisco Sour. Blending citrus juices, as we have here, really helps the depth of flavour.

2 MEASURES LIGHT RUM

½ MEASURE LEMON JUICE

½ MEASURE LIME JUICE

1 MEASURE SUGAR SYRUP

½ MEASURE EGG WHITE

2 DASHES ANGOSTURA BITTERS

LIME WEDGE, TO GARNISH

Add all the ingredients to your cocktail shaker and "dry shake" without ice for 10 seconds, then take the shaker apart and add cubed ice.
Shake vigorously and strain into an old-fashioned glass filled with cubed ice.
Garnish with a lime wedge.

RUSSIAN SPRING PUNCH

Another Dick Bradsell classic created for a society party in the 1980s. Beautifully simple, elegant and deceptively strong. Great at a party.

1½ MEASURES VODKA

¾ MEASURE LEMON JUICE

2 TSP CRÈME DE CASSIS

2 TSP CRÈME DE FRAMBOISE

2 TSP SUGAR SYRUP

CHILLED CHAMPAGNE, TO TOP

TO GARNISH

LEMON SLICE

RASPBERRY

BLACKBERRY

Add all the ingredients except the Champagne to your cocktail shaker, shake and strain into a highball glass filled with crushed ice. Top with Champagne and garnish with a slice of lemon, a raspberry and a blackberry.

RUSTY NAIL

A Scottish classic, around since the 1940s and the perfect cocktail for a whisky lover. Drambuie is a whisky-based herb and honey liqueur, so we are stirring whisky into whisky.

2 MEASURES SCOTCH WHISKY

1 MEASURE DRAMBUIE

LEMON TWIST, TO GARNISH

Add both ingredients to an old-fashioned glass filled with cubed ice.
Stir briefly, and garnish with a lemon twist.

RYE

As with bourbon, the mash bill of American rye whiskey contains corn, rye and malted barley – but by law that mash bill must be made up of at least 51% rye. Originally produced in the north east of the country in the early 1800s, it is spicier, fruitier and more versatile than bourbon, making it ideal for whiskey-based classic cocktails.

"One should not drink much, but often."

Henri de Toulouse-Lautrec

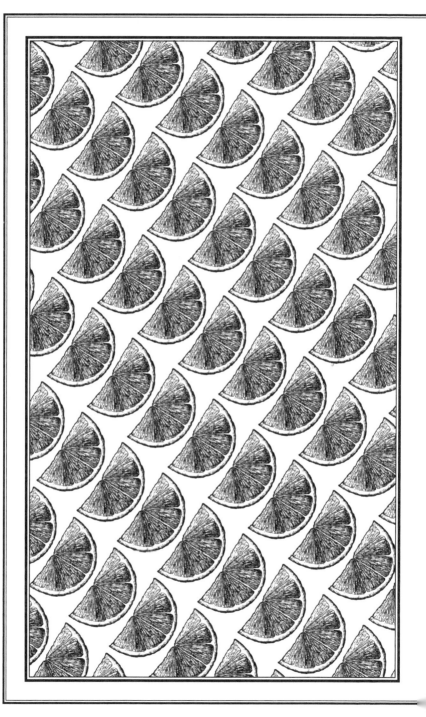

S

SAKE MARTINI

SANGRIA

SATAN'S WHISKERS

SBAGLIATO

SCOTTISH WHISKY

SCREWDRIVER

SEA BREEZE

SEX ON THE BEACH

SIDECAR

SINGAPORE SLING

SLOE GIN SOUR

SOUR

SOUTHSIDE

SOUTH OF THE BORDER

SPARKLING WINE

SPEAKEASY

SPRITZ

STINGER

STRAWBERRY AND MINT
DAIQUIRI

SURFACE TO AIR COCKTAIL

SAKE MARTINI

Wonderfully crisp and citric; notes of gently fermented rice from the sake make for a surprising yet satisfying alternative to the classic Vodka Martini.

2 MEASURES SAKE

1 MEASURE VODKA

½ MEASURE PEACH LIQUEUR

1 DASH ORANGE BITTERS

CUCUMBER RIBBONS, TO GARNISH

Add all ingredients to a cocktail shaker or mixing glass filled with cubed ice, and stir for 30 seconds. Strain into a chilled Martini glass and garnish with cucumber ribbons.

SANGRIA

MAKES 1 JUG

Sangria is simply the name given to the Spanish version of the humble red wine punch, a

European tradition dating back centuries. A Sangria recipe should be instinctive and personal, particularly in your choice of fruit – the recipe below is a great starting point.

1 BOTTLE SPANISH RED WINE
2 MEASURES BRANDY
GINGER ALE, TO TOP
SEASONAL FRUIT, PLUS EXTRA TO GARNISH
MINT SPRIGS, PLUS EXTRA TO GARNISH

Pour the red wine and brandy into a jug filled with cubed ice, top with ginger ale and stir in seasonal fruit and mint sprigs.
Serve in wine glasses with extra mint and fruit.

SATAN'S WHISKERS

Conceived by Harry Craddock, first published in "The Savoy Cocktail Book" (1930). A richer take on the Bronx cocktail, wickedly named and sharp to the taste.

1½ MEASURES GIN
½ MEASURE ORANGE CURAÇAO
½ MEASURE SWEET VERMOUTH
½ MEASURE DRY VERMOUTH
1½ MEASURES ORANGE JUICE
2 DASHES ORANGE BITTERS

Add all the ingredients to your cocktail shaker, shake vigorously and double strain into a chilled coupette glass. No garnish.

SBAGLIATO

A "sbagliato" in Italian might be (politely) translated as "mistake". Created when a busy bartender in Milan poured Prosecco instead of gin while preparing a Negroni. Soft, sparkling and approachable, what a wonderful sbagliato he made.

1 MEASURE CAMPARI

1 MEASURE SWEET VERMOUTH

2 MEASURES CHILLED PROSECCO

ORANGE SLICE, TO GARNISH

Add the ingredients to a rocks glass filled with cubed ice, stir briefly and garnish with a slice of orange.

SCOTTISH WHISKY

Uisege beatha, or "the water of life", was the Celtic name for what we now know as Scottish whisky. As with all spirits, to locate its specific origin would be impossible – but its first recording appears in The Exchequer Rolls of Scotland in 1495. It is an aged spirit derived from either barley or grain, and is identified by region, those regions being Highland, Lowland, Islay, Island, Campbeltown and Speyside, each with unique characteristics of flavour and production.

SCREWDRIVER

The disputed origins of the Screwdriver will never mask the simple fact that this is vodka mixed with orange juice, but its position as a cultural icon is indisputable. Wonderful when made with freshly squeezed orange juice.

2 MEASURES VODKA

5 MEASURES FRESHLY SQUEEZED ORANGE JUICE

ORANGE SLICE, TO GARNISH

Add the ingredients to a highball glass filled with ice. Stir, and garnish with a slice of orange.

SEA BREEZE

As much a mid-century marketing tool for brands of cranberry juice as anything else, the Sea Breeze remains a summer favourite on the west coast of the United States.

2 MEASURES VODKA

2 MEASURES CRANBERRY JUICE

2 MEASURES PINK GRAPEFRUIT
JUICE

LIME WEDGE, TO GARNISH

Add the ingredients to a
highball glass filled with ice.
Stir, and garnish with a lime
wedge.

SEX ON THE BEACH

*Fruited silliness from the 1980s,
provocatively named and sickly
sweet. As enjoyable to say as it
is to drink.*

1 MEASURE VODKA

1 MEASURE PEACH LIQUEUR

1½ MEASURES CRANBERRY
JUICE

1½ MEASURES ORANGE JUICE

ORANGE SLICE, TO GARNISH

Add all the ingredients to
your cocktail shaker, shake
vigorously and strain into
a highball glass filled with
cubed ice.
Garnish with an orange slice.

SIDECAR

*As with most classic cocktails,
the origins of the Sidecar are
unclear, with conflicting sources
between London and Paris
claiming its ownership
throughout the 1920s. What is
beyond dispute, however, is the
drink's enduring quality.
Spectacular.*

1½ MEASURES COGNAC

¾ MEASURE COINTREAU

¾ MEASURE LEMON JUICE, PLUS
EXTRA FOR FROSTING

CASTER SUGAR, FOR FROSTING

LEMON TWIST, TO GARNISH

Dip the rim of a chilled
coupette glass in lemon juice,
and then in caster sugar to

create a sugar frosting around half of the glass.

Then add all ingredients to your cocktail shaker, shake vigorously and double strain into the prepared coupette. Garnish with a lemon twist.

SINGAPORE SLING

Created at the Raffles Hotel in Singapore in the early 1900s. Over the years, pineapple juice has crept into the recipe and, while perfectly permissible, the recipe below is closer to the original.

1 MEASURE GIN

1 MEASURE COINTREAU

½ MEASURE BÉNÉDICTINE

½ MEASURE CHERRY BRANDY

¾ LEMON JUICE

SODA WATER, TO TOP

TO GARNISH

LEMON WEDGE

COCKTAIL CHERRY

Add all ingredients except the soda water to your cocktail shaker.

Shake vigorously and strain into a hurricane glass filled with cubed ice and top with soda water.

Garnish with a wedge of lemon and cocktail cherry.

SLOE GIN SOUR

A fantastic expression of the Gin Sour, given savoury depth from the hedgerow-fruit astringency of sloe gin.

2 MEASURES SLOE GIN

1 MEASURE LEMON JUICE

1 MEASURE SUGAR SYRUP

½ MEASURE EGG WHITE

2 DASHES PEYCHAUD'S BITTERS

ORANGE SLICE, TO GARNISH

Add all the ingredients to your cocktail shaker and "dry shake" without ice for 10 seconds, then take the shaker apart and add cubed ice. Shake vigorously and double strain into an old-fashioned glass filled with cubed ice. Garnish with an orange slice.

SOUR

Sours are cocktails containing a base spirit, citrus and a sweetener, and were first described by Jerry Thomas in his 1862 book "How to Mix Drinks". Derived from the basic principles of punch-making, Sours are the building blocks of cocktail creation: a Margarita is a Sour, a Daiquiri is a Sour... Egg white is often used to assist aeration, giving the cocktail a fluffy, velvet-like texture.

SOUTHSIDE

Most likely a product of Prohibition, when flavourings and sweeteners were required to mask the rough edges of poorly made "bathtub" gin. Fresh and lively.

2 MEASURES GIN

¾ MEASURE LIME JUICE

¾ MEASURE SUGAR SYRUP

6 MINT LEAVES, PLUS EXTRA

LEAF TO GARNISH

Add all the ingredients to your cocktail shaker, shake vigorously and double strain into a chilled coupette glass. Garnish with a mint leaf.

SOUTH OF THE BORDER

A snappy tequila sipper, sitting somewhere between an Old Fashioned and an Espresso Martini.

2 MEASURES TEQUILA

¾ MEASURE KAHLÚA

Add both ingredients to an old-fashioned glass filled with cubed ice and stir briefly.
No garnish.

SPARKLING WINE

Champagne will always spring to mind when we think of sparkling wine, but the category itself is now more broadly reflective of the resourcefulness of the European wine making tradition. Today, Prosecco – originally produced from the "Glera" grape – tops the pile. In part for its relative affordability by comparison to Champagne and its ready availability, but really due to its versatility, uncomplicated and pleasant flavour profile – striking a crisp balance between dry and sweet – it's the new kid on the block, that's always been here.

SPEAKEASY

Also known as "blind pigs", speakeasies were illegal underground drinking dens where patrons had to speak quietly, or "easy", for fear of being discovered. They rose to great prominence during the Prohibition era (1920–1933)

in North America and have been celebrated by popular culture ever since. Dens of glamour and iniquity – those were the days.

SPRITZ

The concept of the Spritz began in Austrian-occupied Italy in the 1800s, when the Habsburg soldiers found the local wine in Veneto too varied, complex and strong for their tastes, and so diluted it with soda water. Over time the Italians adopted the convention, and improved the idea by subtly adding their own bitter vermouths and spirits, creating complex, refreshing and low-alcohol drinks that are now adored the world over.

STINGER

A "stinging", mint-laced after-dinner cocktail from Harry Craddock, first published in "The Savoy Cocktail Book" (1930).

2 MEASURES COGNAC

½ MEASURE CRÈME DE MENTHE

MINT LEAF, TO GARNISH

Add all the ingredients to your cocktail shaker, shake vigorously and double strain into a chilled Martini glass. Garnish with a mint leaf.

STRAWBERRY AND MINT DAIQUIRI

An extremely popular variation of the Cuban classic. All sweetness and sharpness, and pretty to look at.

2 MEASURES WHITE RUM

1 MEASURE LIME JUICE

¾ MEASURE SUGAR SYRUP

4 WHOLE STRAWBERRIES, PLUS A SLICED STRAWBERRY TO GARNISH

5 MINT LEAVES, PLUS AN EXTRA LEAF TO GARNISH

Add all the ingredients to your cocktail shaker, shake vigorously and double strain into a chilled Martini glass. Garnish with a mint leaf and sliced strawberry.

SURFACE TO AIR COCKTAIL

An enticing Coconut Daiquiri, with hints of tropical pineapple and refreshing mint. Apparently devised in the bath by London bartender of note, Liam Cotter at Highwater, Dalston, in 2015.

1 MEASURE COCONUT RUM

1 MEASURE GIN

¾ LIME JUICE

½ MEASURE FRESH PINEAPPLE JUICE

½ MEASURE SUGAR SYRUP

8 MINT LEAVES

Add all the ingredients to your cocktail shaker, shake vigorously and double strain into a chilled coupette glass. No garnish.

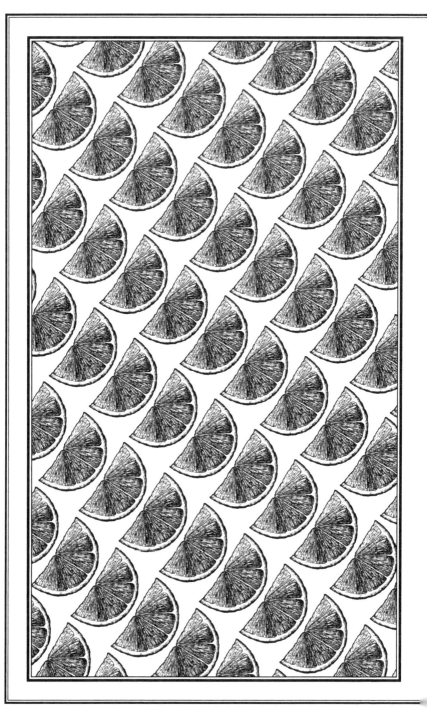

T

TEQUILA SUNRISE

A colourful way of sweetening tequila and orange juice, though the original recipe may well have contained crème de cassis as opposed to grenadine. A kitsch holiday favourite to sip in the evening sun.

2 MEASURES GOLD TEQUILA
4 MEASURES FRESH ORANGE JUICE
2 TSP GRENADINE
ORANGE SLICE, TO GARNISH

Add the tequila and orange juice to a hurricane glass filled with cubed ice. Carefully drizzle the grenadine over the top of the drink, so that it bleeds through to create a sunrise effect, and garnish with a slice of orange.

TEXAS TEA

A perky alternative to the classic Long Island Iced Tea. Any fruited tea will work well, and is essential in bringing these complex flavours together.

1 MEASURE TEQUILA

1 MEASURE WHITE RUM

½ MEASURE COINTREAU

½ MEASURE SUGAR SYRUP

½ MEASURE LEMON JUICE

1 MEASURE ORANGE JUICE

2 MEASURES COLD FRUIT TEA

TO GARNISH

ORANGE SLICE

LEMON SLICE

MINT SPRIG

Add all the ingredients to your cocktail shaker, shake vigorously and strain into a hurricane glass filled with cubed ice.
Garnish with slice of orange and lemon, and a mint sprig.

TIKI
The word "Tiki" hails from the depths of Polynesian mythology, and was loosely and flamboyantly appropriated in North America in the 1930s. The term covers an entire aesthetic and liquid style: bright colours and tropical ingredients, Hawaiian shirts and cocktail umbrellas. The founding fathers were two larger-than-life Californians, Donn "Don the Beachcomber" Beach and Victor "Trader Vic" Bergeron, whose friendly, and arguably contrived, rivalry defined the era as much as the cocktails themselves.

TIPPERARY

*Conflicting recipes for Tipperary appear in print from the beginning of the 20th century. It takes the concept of the Manhattan cocktail as a starting point, but roots itself in the headier sweet notes of Irish whiskey, with green Chartreuse providing herbal spice.
Complex, but rewarding.*

1½ MEASURES IRISH WHISKEY

¾ MEASURE SWEET VERMOUTH

½ MEASURE GREEN
CHARTREUSE

2 DASHES ORANGE BITTERS

COCKTAIL CHERRY, TO
GARNISH

Add all the ingredients to
a cocktail shaker or mixing
glass filled with cubed ice.
Stir for 30 seconds and strain
into a chilled coupette glass.
Garnish with a cocktail
cherry.

¾ MEASURE SUGAR SYRUP

SODA WATER, TO TOP

TO GARNISH

LEMON WEDGE

COCKTAIL CHERRY

Pour the gin, lemon juice,
sugar syrup and a splash of
soda water into a highball
glass.
Fill the glass with cubed ice
and stir, top with soda water
and more ice and garnish
with a lemon wedge and a
cocktail cherry.

TOM COLLINS

*Appearing first in print in Jerry
Thomas's "The Bartender's
Guide" (1876), though most
likely much older; so named
because the original recipe
would have called for Old Tom
Gin, a sweeter style than
London Dry Gin. Timeless,
refreshing and elegant.*

2 MEASURES GIN

1 MEASURE LEMON JUICE

TOMMY'S
MARGARITA

*A contemporary interpretation
of the classic Margarita created
at Tommy's Bar in San
Francisco in 1990. The
sweetness of agave can be
difficult to balance, so ensure
you measure accurately.*

2 MEASURES GOLD TEQUILA

1 MEASURE LIME JUICE

2 TSP AGAVE SYRUP

LIME WEDGE, TO GARNISH

Add all the ingredients to your cocktail shaker, shake vigorously and strain into a rocks glass filled with cubed ice.
Garnish with a lime wedge.

Add all the ingredients to your cocktail shaker, shake vigorously and strain into an old-fashioned glass filled with cubed ice.
Garnish with slice of lime, a cocktail cherry and a mint sprig.

TRADER VIC'S MAI TAI

Created by Victor Jules Bergeron, or "Trader Vic", in 1944 at his Polynesian restaurant in Oakland, California. Lying somewhere between a Daiquiri and a Margarita, but sweetened with almond, when made well the Mai Tai is one of those drinks that cannot fail to make you happy.

1½ MEASURES GOLD RUM

¾ MEASURE COINTREAU

¾ MEASURE LIME JUICE

2 TSP ORGEAT

1 TSP SUGAR SYRUP

TO GARNISH

LIME SLICE

COCKTAIL CHERRY

MINT SPRIG

TRINIDAD SOUR

There is no mistake written below; you are reading 1 measure of Angostura bitters correctly. Giuseppe Gonzalez's outrageous creation, fearsomely flavoured yet perfectly balanced, is one for the adventurous.

½ MEASURE RYE WHISKEY

1 MEASURE ANGOSTURA BITTERS

1 MEASURE LEMON JUICE

1 MEASURE ORGEAT

Add all the ingredients to your cocktail shaker, shake vigorously and strain into a chilled coupette glass.
No garnish.

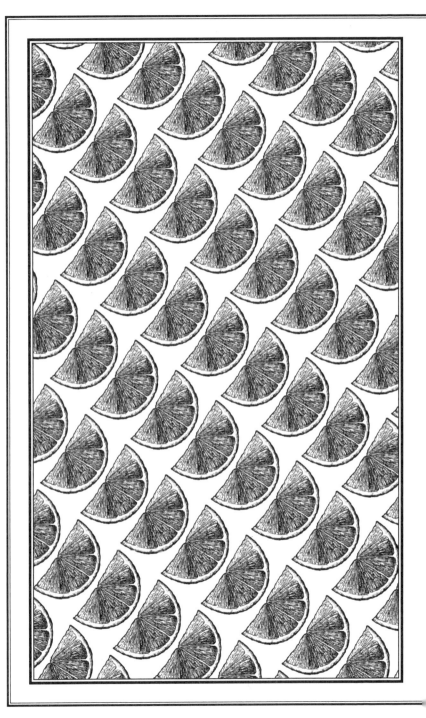

ULTIMATE IRISH COFFEE

VALENTINE MARTINI

VANILLA FIX

VESPER MARTINI

VIEUX CARRÉ

VODKA

VODKA GIBSON

VODKA SOUR

ULTIMATE IRISH COFFEE

The epitome of indulgence, and a naughty favourite of many, this is worth taking the time to prepare properly. Everyone will have their preferred recipe and the one below, though a little more complex than some, will not disappoint.

1½ MEASURES IRISH WHISKEY

½ MEASURE COFFEE LIQUEUR

1 MEASURE VANILLA SYRUP

2 MEASURES ESPRESSO

WHIPPED CREAM, TO TOP

Gently heat the ingredients in a small saucepan till warm, but not boiling.
Pour into a rocks glass and top with whipped cream.

VALENTINE MARTINI

A sharply flavoured Raspberry Martini, with a brisk vodka kick, and perfectly enjoyable on occasions other than Valentine's Day.

2 MEASURES RASPBERRY VODKA

¾ MEASURE LIME JUICE

½ MEASURE SUGAR SYRUP

6 RASPBERRIES, PLUS EXTRA TO GARNISH

LIME TWIST, TO GARNISH

Add all the ingredients to your cocktail shaker, shake vigorously and double strain into a chilled Martini glass. Garnish with raspberries and a twist of lime.

VANILLA FIX

Vanilla complements bourbon beautifully in this sweet and floral Whiskey Fix.

2 MEASURES BOURBON WHISKEY

1 MEASURE LEMON JUICE

¾ MEASURE VANILLA SYRUP

1 TSP GRENADINE

COCKTAIL CHERRIES, TO GARNISH

Add all the ingredients except the grenadine to your cocktail shaker. Shake vigorously and double strain into a rocks glass filled with crushed ice, then gently drizzle the grenadine over the top. Crown with more crushed ice and garnish with cocktail cherries.

VESPER MARTINI

The only truly acceptable occasion when a Martini is shaken – and derived straight from the pages of Ian Fleming's first James Bond novel, "Casino Royale" (1953). A vigorous shake and the addition of lillet blanc dilute, soften and freshen.

2½ MEASURES GIN

1 MEASURE VODKA

½ MEASURE LILLET BLANC

LEMON TWIST, TO GARNISH

Add all the ingredients to the bottom of your cocktail shaker, and fill the top half of it with ice. Shake vigorously and double

strain into a chilled Martini glass.
Garnish with a lemon twist.

VIEUX CARRÉ

A New Orleans classic. Almost a Manhattan and almost an Old Fashioned, this exemplifies the very best of traditional American drinks–making. Highly recommended.

1 MEASURE RYE WHISKEY

1 MEASURE COGNAC

1 MEASURE SWEET VERMOUTH

1 TSP BÉNÉDICTINE

2 DASHES ANGOSTURA BITTERS

ORANGE TWIST, TO GARNISH

Add all of the ingredients to an old-fashioned glass filled with cubed ice.
Stir briefly, and garnish with an orange twist.

VODKA
Vodka's origins lie in Poland, where there are mentions of "wodka" or "little water" in court documents from the year 1405. A crude product – vodka is an unaged grain spirit distilled from rye, corn, wheat or potato, to name the most common base crops. It is often, sadly, seen as inferior or tasteless when compared to the other major spirit categories, but the sheer clarity and simplicity of a well-made vodka is the truest expression of artisan skill.

VODKA GIBSON

The alternative to the classic Gibson, with vodka bringing lighter and creamier citrus notes to this most drinkable of Dry Martinis. And do remember, there is no such thing as a Gibson with too many onions.

2½ MEASURES VODKA

½ MEASURE DRY VERMOUTH

COCKTAIL ONIONS, TO GARNISH

Add the vodka and dry vermouth to a cocktail shaker or mixing glass, and fill with cubed ice. Stir for 30 seconds, and strain into a chilled Martini glass. Garnish generously with cocktail onions.

and add cubed ice. Shake vigorously and double strain into an old-fashioned glass filled with cubed ice. Garnish with a lemon wedge and a cocktail cherry.

VODKA SOUR

An elegant Sour for vodka lovers, or lovers of good drinks, to be quite honest. Vibrant and zesty, use the best-quality vodka you can to really enjoy it to its fullest potential.

2 MEASURES VODKA

1 MEASURE LEMON JUICE

¾ MEASURE SUGAR SYRUP

½ MEASURE EGG WHITE

1 DASH ORANGE BITTERS

TO GARNISH

LEMON WEDGE

COCKTAIL CHERRY

Add all the ingredients to your shaker and "dry shake" without ice for 10 seconds, then take the shaker apart

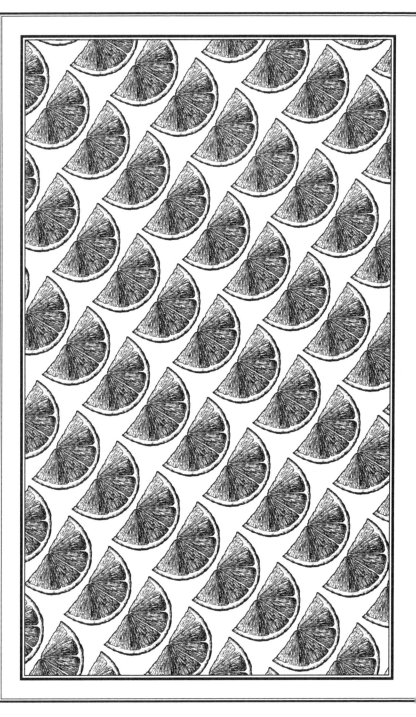

W

WATERMELON PUNCH

MAKES 1 JUG

Rich summer fruit and thirst-quenching watermelon make this the perfect summer sharer with friends. Sunshine in a glass.

4 MEASURES VODKA

2 MEASURES STRAWBERRY LIQUEUR

8 MEASURES WATERMELON JUICE

2 MEASURES LIME JUICE

1 MEASURE SUGAR SYRUP

1 HANDFUL TORN MINT LEAVES

TO GARNISH

WATERMELON SLICES

STRAWBERRIES

MINT SPRIGS

Add all the ingredients to a jug or punch bowl filled with cubed ice and stir well. Garnish with slices of watermelon, strawberries and sprigs of mint and serve in wine glasses.

WHISKEY SOUR

Silky smooth and perfectly balanced. Rich bourbon and sharp citrus make this classic Whiskey Sour formula one to be made time and time again. Easy on the egg, heavy on the bitters. Delicious.

2 MEASURES BOURBON WHISKEY

1 MEASURE LEMON JUICE

¾ MEASURE SUGAR SYRUP

½ MEASURE EGG WHITE

2 DASHES ANGOSTURA BITTERS

TO GARNISH

LEMON WEDGE

COCKTAIL CHERRY

Add all the ingredients to your shaker and "dry shake" without ice for 10 seconds, then take the shaker apart and add cubed ice.
Shake vigorously and double strain into an old-fashioned glass filled with cubed ice.
Garnish with a lemon wedge and a cocktail cherry.

WHISKY MAC

Attributed to Colonel Hector MacDonald, who is said to have created it while serving in India during the time of the British Raj. A perfect blend of honeyed complexity and sharp ginger, a winter drink for a summer day.

2 MEASURES SCOTCH WHISKY

1 MEASURE GINGER WINE

Pour the whisky and ginger wine into an old-fashioned glass filled with cubed ice and stir briefly.
No garnish.

WHISKY OR WHISKEY?

The spelling of whisky, or whiskey, is determined by where it is made. As a general rule it is whiskey in America and Ireland, whereas whisky is preferred in Scotland, Canada and the rest of the world. In the late 1800s, Scottish whisky was of a relatively poor quality, so Irish distillers wanted to differentiate what they were exporting to North America, by adding an "e" – endlessly confusing.

WHITE LADY

Essentially a Sidecar made with gin, argument raged between Harry MacElhone and Harry Craddock as to who created this evergreen classic. Logic and chronology would suggest is was MacElhone, though the recipe below is nearer to Craddock's drier version, published in "The Savoy Cocktail Book" (1930).

1½ MEASURES GIN

1 MEASURE COINTREAU

¾ MEASURE LEMON JUICE

LEMON TWIST, TO GARNISH

Add all the ingredients to your cocktail shaker, shake vigorously and double strain into a chilled coupette glass. Garnish with a lemon twist.

WHITE NEGRONI

A floral and far softer modern interpretation of the Italian classic. Training wheels for the real thing if you find the bitter flavours of the original a touch challenging; very pleasant indeed.

1 MEASURE GIN

1 MEASURE DRY VERMOUTH

1 MEASURE COCCHI AMERICANO

LEMON SLICE, TO GARNISH

Pour all the ingredients into a rocks glass filled with ice. Stir briefly, and garnish with a lemon slice.

WHITE RUSSIAN

Russian in a no way, indulgent in every way. Rich, creamy and silly, it returned to modern parlance thanks to the film "The Big Lebowski". Ideally drunk with a knowing sense of nostalgia.

1 MEASURE VODKA

1 MEASURE COFFEE LIQUEUR

1 MEASURE WHOLE MILK

1 MEASURE SINGLE CREAM

Pour the coffee liqueur into a rocks glass filled with crushed ice.
Then add the remaining ingredients to your cocktail shaker, shake vigorously and strain into the glass, creating a layered effect.
No garnish.

4 MEASURES ORANGE JUICE

ORANGE SLICE, TO GARNISH

Add all ingredients to your cocktail shaker, shake vigorously and strain into a highball glass.
Garnish with slices of orange.

WOODSTOCK

An enlivened Gin and Orange, pleasantly dry with citric floral notes.

1½ MEASURES GIN

1 MEASURE DRY VERMOUTH

½ MEASURE COINTREAU

½ MEASURE LEMON JUICE

2 TBSP SUGAR SYRUP

X
Y
Z

XYZ COCKTAIL

YALE COCKTAIL

ZOMBIE

ZOMBIE

XYZ COCKTAIL

A simple, potent and thoroughly satisfying Rum Sidecar. First appearing in print in "The Savoy Cocktail Book" (1930), though most likely predating it. Snappy and drinkable.

1½ MEASURES AGED RUM
1 MEASURE COINTREAU
½ MEASURE LEMON JUICE

Add all ingredients to your cocktail shaker, shake vigorously and strain into a highball glass.
No garnish.

YALE COCKTAIL

A Gin Martini with the additional touch of maraschino, which gives an astringent, fruited complexity. Originating from the famed Ivy League College of the same name.

2 MEASURES GIN

¾ MEASURE DRY VERMOUTH

2 TBSP MARASCHINO

2 DASHES ORANGE BITTERS

LEMON TWIST, TO GARNISH

Add all the ingredients to
a cocktail shaker or mixing
glass, and fill with cubed ice.
Stir for 30 seconds and strain
into a chilled Martini glass.
Garnish with a lemon twist.

ZOMBIE

Legend would have it that Donn Beach (or "Don the Beachcomber") created the Zombie for a particularly hungover customer to aid his recovery before a business engagement in Los Angeles in the mid-1930s. When the customer returned days later, to complain that the drink in question had turned him into a "Zombie", a Tiki classic was born. A clever blend of fruit masks the ludicrous potency of this benchmark rum punch.

ZOMBIE

This is a fearsomely potent rum punch, so potent in fact that in most reputable cocktail bars customers would usually be restricted to just one of them. The recipe has changed over time, the basic idea being that fruit makes the riotous blend of rums palatable. The below reflects the sense of "Don the Beachcomber's" initial intentions. Do be careful.

1½ MEASURES LIGHT RUM

1½ MEASURES DARK RUM

½ MEASURE VELVET FALERNUM

½ MEASURE OVERPROOF RUM

¾ MEASURE LIME JUICE

½ MEASURE GRENADINE

2 MEASURES GRAPEFRUIT JUICE

2 DASHES ABSINTHE

1 DASH ANGOSTURA BITTERS

TO GARNISH

LIME SLICES

COCKTAIL CHERRIES

MINT SPRIGS

Add all ingredients to
your cocktail shaker, shake
vigorously and strain into a
hurricane glass (or Tiki mug
if you have one) filled with
crushed ice.
Garnish extravagantly with
lime slices, cocktail cherries,
mint sprigs and anything else
you like.

INDEX